NEW VANGUARD 317

BRITISH AIRCRAFT CARRIERS 1945–2010

ANGUS KONSTAM   ILLUSTRATED BY PAUL WRIGHT

OSPREY PUBLISHING
Bloomsbury Publishing Plc
Kemp House, Chawley Park, Cumnor Hill, Oxford OX2 9PH, UK
29 Earlsfort Terrace, Dublin 2, Ireland
1385 Broadway, 5th Floor, New York, NY 10018, USA
E-mail: info@ospreypublishing.com
www.ospreypublishing.com

OSPREY is a trademark of Osprey Publishing Ltd

First published in Great Britain in 2023

A catalogue record for this book is available from the British Library.

ISBN: PB 9781472856876; eBook 9781472856890

ePDF 9781472856906; XML 9781472856883

23 24 25 26 27 10 9 8 7 6 5 4 3 2 1

Index by Alan Rutter
Typeset by PDQ Digital Media Solutions, Bungay, UK
Printed and bound in India by Replika Press Private Ltd.

Osprey Publishing supports the Woodland Trust, the UK's leading woodland
conservation charity.

To find out more about our authors and books visit
www.ospreypublishing.com. Here you will find extracts, author
interviews, details of forthcoming events and the option to sign up for our
newsletter.

All photos courtesy of the Stratford Archive

Title page image: HMS *Illustrious*, the namesake of her three-ship class,
was one of Britain's most famous wartime carriers, but she remained in
service for another decade after the war, performing the role of the fleet's
trials carrier. As such she was the vital testbed for the Royal Navy's
immediate post-war generation of jet-age aircraft.

CONTENTS

BRITISH AIRCRAFT CARRIERS 1945–2010

INTRODUCTION

By August 1945, the Royal Navy possessed a potent carrier strike force of nine carriers, most of which were concentrated in the Pacific. This was arguably the most powerful task group ever assembled in the Navy's long history. Back home, over twice as many new carriers were under construction, while a new generation of jet aircraft was beginning to enter service. While this carrier force was smaller than that of the US Navy, in the immediate aftermath of the war the future for Britain's carrier fleet looked reasonably bright.

This, however, didn't account for the dire state of Britain's post-war economy. Inevitably, many of the carriers under construction were cancelled, while naval funding was reduced, leading to further cuts in the carrier fleet. Many of Britain's war-built carriers also needed extensive modification to make them suitable for jet aircraft. Still, during the decade after the war, Britain developed new carrier technology such as steam catapults, angled flight decks and mirrored landing aids. These all made their carriers better suited to the operation of jet aircraft. At the same time, the Cold War threat posed by the Soviet submarine fleet led to the conversion of several existing ships into anti-submarine carriers.

During the decades that followed, the Navy had to adapt to its more limited global role, and a greater emphasis on Britain's NATO (North Atlantic Treaty Organization) commitments within Atlantic waters. At the same time, plans to build new carriers were thwarted by the parsimony of successive British governments. As a result, by the 1970s it was decided to decommission the Navy's carrier fleet, and instead to concentrate on anti-submarine warfare (ASW). This led to the loss of fixed-wing carriers by the end of the decade, and the development of a new class of light ASW carriers. The demise of conventional carriers however, revealed a need for air assets capable of accompanying a British task force. This gap was filled by the adaptation of the light carriers to operate the Sea Harrier.

The island of *Eagle* in the mid-1950s, pictured before her modernization in 1959–61. In the foreground is a Fairey Gannet AS1 of 826 NAS, which had just replaced the Grumman Avengers of 815 NAS as the carrier's embarked ASW squadron.

These ably proved their worth during the Falklands War (1982) and led to a reprieve for fixed-wing naval aviation until the Harrier's retirement from service in 2006, and the subsequent decommissioning of Britain's remaining light carriers. Still, the need for the long-range projection of naval power remained, and so, in 1998, plans were developed for a new generation of British aircraft carriers. However, it would be almost two decades before these carriers entered service. In the meantime, in 2014, the Navy lost its last carrier. The retiral of the Sea Harrier led to almost a decade-long hiatus in fixed-wing naval aviation. This ending of an era then, and the gap between the beginning of a new one, provides us with an opportunity to take stock of the Royal Navy's post-war achievements in carrier operation, raised to a peak of excellence before a lack of government understanding brought this dramatic era to a close.

HMS *Eagle*, pictured in the mid-1950s. An Attacker is ranged on her starboard catapults, while other Attackers (800 and 803 NAS), as well as Fireflies (814), Sea Hornets (809) and Skyraider AEWs (849C NAS) are parked at the after end of her flight deck.

DESIGN AND DEVELOPMENT

At the end of World War II, Britain boasted an impressively powerful carrier fleet. Including its numerous escort carriers, the Royal Navy had 50 aircraft carriers in service, with another 18 under construction. Those in commission included the six Illustrious-, Indomitable- and Implacable-class fleet carriers, five Colossus-class light fleet carriers and 38 escort carriers. It also included the maintenance ship *Unicorn*, which could embark aircraft when required.

Another fleet carrier, the badly ageing *Furious*, had been placed in reserve. On the stocks were three Eagle-class fleet carriers, five more of the Colossus class (two of which would also be maintenance ships), and ten more Majestic- and Centaur-class light carriers. In addition, plans had been drawn up for another four Centaurs, and four Malta-class fleet carriers. Peace, however, brought an end to the government's open purse and Lend-Lease aid.

The post-war carrier force
This meant a dramatic and immediate scaling back of the British fleet. The first victims were those of the Malta class, whose orders were cancelled. So too were four of the Centaur class, while completion of the rest was postponed. One of the Eagle class was cancelled while under construction, while work on the remaining two was delayed. All six of the Majestics were now earmarked for sale or transfer to other navies, along with two of the Colossus class. *Furious* was sold for scrap, being broken up in 1948. All 32 of the surviving Lend-Lease escort carriers were returned to the United States, while five of the six British-built escort carriers were sold off. The last of them, *Campania*, was placed in reserve, and was finally scrapped in 1955. Of the remaining carriers, many were in need of a refit, and were generally deemed unsuitable for the new generation of heavy carrier-based aircraft.

The result was that by the start of the Korean War in June 1950, the Royal Navy only had four operational aircraft carriers: *Implacable*

and *Theseus* serving in home waters, *Glory* in the Mediterranean and *Triumph* in the Far East. Of the others, some were in reserve or being refitted, while others were being used for trials, training or even as troop carriers. Even *Implacable*, an operational fleet carrier, was earmarked for the evaluation of the Sea Vampire jet fighter. So, in just five years, the strength of Britain's carrier fleet had been reduced dramatically, while the handful of carriers still under construction had faced a similar cull. Britain's post-war poverty was only part of the reason.

The Colossus-class light carrier *Warrior* in Malta's Grand Harbour, October 1954. At the time, she was returning from her deployment off Korea. Her Sea Furies and Fireflies have been flown off. Four years later she was sold to the Argentinian Navy, becoming the ARA *Independencia*.

Conversions and cancellations

Another problem was the condition of the existing carrier fleet. The armoured fleet carriers had all been damaged during the war, and several still bore their wartime scars. Their limited hangar height and space also made them unsuited to the operation of large propeller-driven or jet aircraft. The initial idea was to modernize them, and in 1950, *Victorious* began an extensive eight-year refit. Plans to upgrade the others were shelved due to cost. In 1946 the Royal Navy decided to complete the building of only six of its new carriers (*Ark Royal*, *Eagle*, *Albion*, *Bulwark*, *Centaur* and *Hermes*). While this move saved money, it also committed the Admiralty to the modernization of these carriers, which had all been designed to suit wartime aircraft, rather than larger post-war ones. Fortuitously though, this also allowed them to be extensively adapted before their completion, to reflect developments in both aircraft and flight deck technology.

The old warhorse of the Mediterranean campaign, HMS *Illustrious*, pictured during a visit to the Channel Islands in 1946. She had just emerged from a post-war refit in Rosyth, and had been re-commissioned as a trials and training carrier. She continued to fulfil this important role until 1954.

As a result, *Albion*, *Bulwark* and *Centaur* were completed with partially angled flight decks and hydraulic catapults, and all three entered service in 1953–54. This preceded the final development of many of these technological improvements, and while *Hermes*, which joined the fleet in 1959, had a steam catapult and a more pronounced 6½° angled flight deck, it was decided not to upgrade her sister ships, with their less powerful catapults and 5½° angled flight decks. Again, post-war parsimony limited the ability of the Royal Navy's carrier strike force. Due to their size, the Centaurs could only operate 26 aircraft, and only *Hermes* could manage larger, heavier jets. So, the decision was made in 1958 to convert *Albion* and *Bulwark* into 'commando carriers', or amphibious assault ships, equipped to carry Wessex helicopters rather than fixed-wing aircraft. This was duly done between 1959 and 1961.

Similarly, *Ark Royal* was completed in 1955 with a partially angled flight deck, but this was improved to 9° in 1960, and was upgraded again in 1969, to accommodate the F4 Phantom jet strike aircraft. Her sister ship, *Eagle*, entered service without an angled deck, but received one during a refit in 1954–55.

In-flight refuelling under way between two Buccaneer S1s of 800 NAS, embarked on HMS *Eagle* during the mid 1960s. The Buccaneer had a relatively limited range of around 500nm, so mid-air refuelling was a useful means of extending its strike radius.

She underwent a much more extensive refit between 1959 and 1964, but she was never further upgraded to carry Phantoms, which limited her long-term effectiveness. This was also the case with *Victorious*, the last of the wartime fleet carriers, which was beginning to show her age by the mid-1960s. At the time, the Royal Navy hoped to keep at least *Eagle* and *Ark Royal* in operation until the mid-1970s, when a new generation of aircraft carriers would replace them. Its hopes were pinned on the CVA-01, the first of a new class of four British attack carriers (CVA).

These would displace over 64,000 tons when fully laden and be capable of carrying up to 50 modern aircraft, including Phantoms and Buccaneers, as well as helicopters and Gannet AEW (airborne early warning) aircraft. The scale of the CVA project was scaled back during the 1960s, and it was eventually cancelled in 1966. While part of the reason was financial, the CVA project had also fallen victim to intense lobbying by the Royal Air Force (RAF). This effectively marked the death knell for the future of Britain's carrier strike force. By then, the operational carrier fleet had been reduced to just four ageing carriers, all of which were expected to be decommissioned by the end of the 1970s. Following the decision, it was decided that the Royal Navy would concentrate on its NATO commitments in the North Atlantic, and leave the business of strategic power projection to the RAF.

This NATO commitment primarily meant a commitment to ASW operations. The Royal Navy made extensive use of helicopters in ASW operations, having abandoned fixed-wing ASW aircraft in 1968. The Wessex III, and later the Sea King, proved ideal for the job, augmenting the smaller helicopters, but these took up space in aircraft carriers, which in turn reduced the vessel's fixed-wing capacity. The solution was to build a through-deck cruiser capable of carrying up to a dozen ASW helicopters. These plans evolved into the Invincible class of light ASW carriers, the first of which entered service in 1980. This coincided with the demise of the larger fixed-wing carriers. *Hermes* had been converted into an ASW carrier in 1977, by which time *Eagle* and *Ark Royal* were due to be decommissioned. The end for the two carriers came in 1978–79.

By this time, the decision had been made to adapt both *Hermes* and the Invincible-class carriers, so they could operate the Sea Harrier. This gave the Fleet Air Arm a reprieve, and so, when Argentina invaded the Falkland Islands in 1982, the Royal Navy had two operational light carriers – *Hermes* and *Invincible*. The success of the Sea Harrier during the Falklands War guaranteed the future of both the light carriers and their air wings. *Hermes* though, was at the end of her useful life, and was decommissioned in 1984, and sold to the Indian Navy two years later. After the Falklands War, the

A Supermarine Scimitar F1 of 803 NAS coming in to land on *Ark Royal*'s angled flight deck, c.1965-66. This one-man strike fighter entered operational service in 1959, and was phased out in 1966, when it was replaced by the Buccaneer.

Invincibles remained in service for another two decades. *Invincible* was finally decommissioned in 2005, a year before the Sea Harrier was retired from service. Her two sister ships then became ASW helicopter carriers, but *Ark Royal* was unexpectedly decommissioned in 2010, followed by *Illustrious* in 2014.

The early retirement of *Ark Royal* was primarily a political decision. In 1998, the previous government had decided to build two new aircraft carriers to improve Britain's ability to assist in global policing. After an extensive design process, which included the sourcing of suitable fixed-wing aircraft, contracts to build two Queen Elizabeth-class carriers were signed in 2008. Two years later, following another Defence Review, the incoming government found it was unable to cancel these contracts, so elected to decommission *Ark Royal* as part of its plan to scale down Britain's armed forces. This meant that, despite a hiatus, the future of Britain's new carrier strike force was secure. Ironically, the two new Queen Elizabeth-class carriers are comparable in terms of size to the CV-01-type carriers which had been axed by another government just over half a century earlier.

Jet-age problems

In 1948, the arrival of the Sea Vampire, the Navy's first jet fighter, marked a new era for naval aviation. It replaced the twin-engined, piston-driven Sea Hornet, a naval version of the Mosquito. While this was an exciting departure for the Fleet Air Arm, it also created problems. Britain's wartime carriers had originally been designed to carry biplanes, and now they had to be adapted to the needs of the jet age. Even the piston-powered aircraft of the late 1940s such as the Sea Fury, Fairey Firefly and Sea Hornet were much heavier than the Swordfish, Fulmar and Albacore embarked in British carriers a decade earlier. They were also faster, which brought its own problems. Accident rates were alarmingly high, and in 1949, these reached a peak of one landing in fifty ending in a crash. It could be argued that this was partly due to the confusion created by the introduction of new deck-landing techniques and

LIGHT CARRIER: *THESEUS* (1950) AND MAINTENANCE CARRIER: *UNICORN* (1951)

1. *Theseus* (R64). The Colossus-class light carrier *Theseus* was completed after the end of the war, and was commissioned in early 1946. During 1946–48 she served with both the Pacific and Home fleets, and in June 1950 was involved in the first night-deck landing by a jet, a Sea Vampire. *Theseus* was then ordered to Korea, embarking an air group (17th CAG) of Sea Furies (807 NAS) and Fireflies (813 NAS). She remained in Korean waters until the following April where her aircraft flew thousands of sorties, attacking bridges, trains, truck convoys and shipping. This illustration shows the carrier in the winter of 1950–51, while attempting to stem the Chinese counter-offensive. Also shown **(1a)** is a Firefly of 813 NAS, in her Korean colour scheme.

2. *Unicorn* (I72). The idea of a maintenance carrier designed to support the carrier-strike fleet was developed during World War II. It served a range of functions, as a depot and repair ship, a transport for replacement aircraft, a training carrier and as a makeshift operational carrier if required. *Unicorn* was actually commissioned in 1943 as an operational carrier and that September saw action off Salerno. By 1945, while serving with the British Pacific Fleet, she had reverted to her maintenance and transport roles and, even though she was placed in reserve (1946), she was recommissioned for the Korean War and spent the conflict supporting the carrier strike group there. One of her major roles was to provide the group with replacement aircraft, like the **(2a)** Sea Fury of 802 NAS shown here.

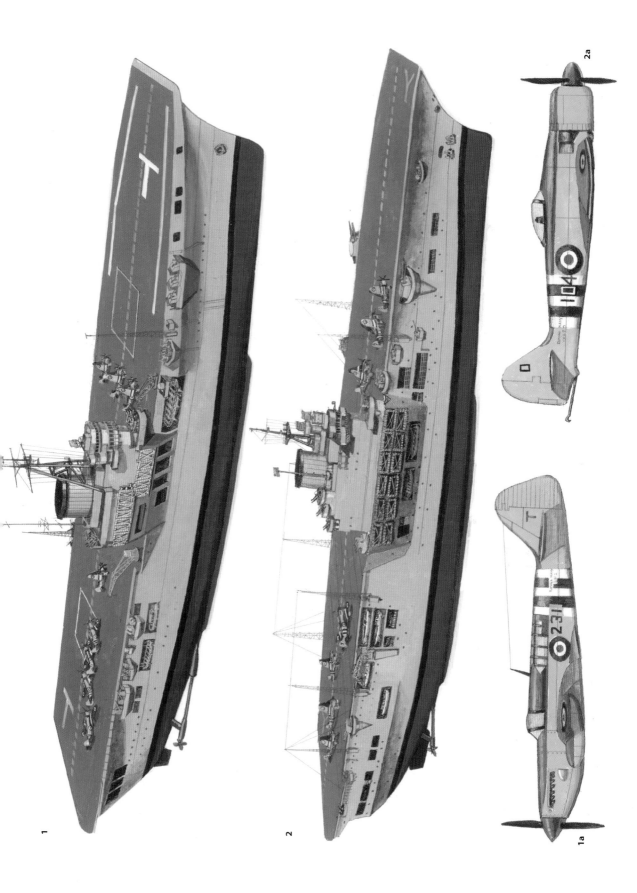

1

2

2a

1a

The Fairey Firefly entered service in 1943 as the replacement for the Fairey Fulmar. It was employed in 24 FAA squadrons, and saw post-war service during the Korean War and the Malay Emergency, before being phased out in 1953–55.

bat signals in 1948–49. However, it was mostly due to the dangers of operating high-performance aircraft on small axial flight decks, which had never been designed for aircraft that powerful.

This, however, helped to spur on the development of a number of technical innovations. Not only would these make carrier operations safer, but they would also give the Royal Navy the tools it needed to handle the increasingly large and potent aircraft of the jet age. The steam catapult, the mirrored landing system and the angled flight deck were all initially developed in Britain, and first tried out on British carriers. However, it would be the US Navy that developed them to their full potential. Together, and with help from evolutionary developments to carrier-borne aircraft, these three technical innovations would allow Britain's post-war aircraft carriers to operate jet aircraft safely and efficiently. In the process, they would ensure that the Royal Navy's carrier fleet had a significant role to play in what was dubbed 'The Cold War'.

The steam catapult

During World War II, the Royal Navy's aircraft carriers used hydraulic catapults to launch their aircraft. In these devices, stored water pressure was rapidly transferred to a catapult shuttle, which was attached to the aircraft. It would then speed down the catapult track, which could be up to 300ft long, before the aircraft was released at the forward end of the flight deck. The H3 catapult fitted to the fleet carriers at the end of the war could launch a 20,000lb aircraft at a speed of 65kts. This was ample force for the piston-engined aircraft of the immediate post-war years, but as larger jet-powered aircraft appeared, it was clear that something more powerful would be needed. The Royal Navy had considered steam-powered catapults before the war, but initial designs were never developed. A similar system had been used by the Germans during the war to launch their V-1 flying bombs.

Aircraft handlers from HMS *Illustrious*, *c.*1950–51. Each aircraft was assigned a handlers team, who were responsible for it when it was brought up on deck. After unfolding the wings, they would then move it on the flight deck as required, or secure it to a steam catapult.

During World War II, Cdr Colin Mitchell RNVR (1904–69), an accomplished marine engineer, had worked for the Admiralty's Engineering Department. When peace came he returned to his native Edinburgh as the technical director of Brown Brothers, a marine engineering company. He examined German designs for the V-1 catapult, along with captured parts, and then set about developing a far more ambitious system, designed to launch naval aircraft. Essentially, the aircraft would be hooked onto a piston, which was housed in a cylinder fitted beneath the flight deck. High-pressure steam from the ship's engines was used to power the piston, and when released it would propel the aircraft along the catapult at high speed, so generating the lift needed for take-off.

Mitchell's prototype was approved for trials by the Admiralty, and in August 1950, it was tested on HMS *Perseus*. It proved highly successful – so much so that the following year *Perseus* crossed the Atlantic to demonstrate Mitchell's catapult to the US Navy. While the British Admiralty prevaricated, in 1952 the US Navy began building its own steam catapults, having negotiated the rights from Brown Brothers. However, it would be 1955 before the Royal Navy first received the company's catapults, which were fitted to the newly built *Ark Royal*. Today, Mitchell's steam catapult is still in widespread use around the world.

A Phantom FG-1 of 892 NAS being launched from the port catapult of *Ark Royal*, *c*.1970. Although American designed, the British variant carried the more powerful Rolls-Royce Spey engine, which gave it an edge in power and speed over its American counterparts. Note the SAR Wessex I deployed off the carrier's port side during the launch.

Incidentally, in 1951 a hydro-pneumatic catapult system was fitted to *Eagle*, which was capable of launching a 30,000lb aircraft at 75kts. Later, it would be replaced by a steam catapult system during her 1959–64 refit.

The angled flight deck

During World War II, the aim of launching and recovering aircraft simultaneously was an attractive proposition, and was partly achieved by dividing the flight deck in two. The forward section was used to launch aircraft, either under their own power or by using hydraulic catapults. A crash barrier separated this from the after portion of the flight deck, which was used for landings. With a reliable arrester wire system, it was possible to catch the aircraft before it reached this dividing barrier. However, if the arrester hook failed to catch them, the aircraft could bounce over the steel mesh barrier, and collide with aircraft ranged for take-off on its far side. Even if the barrier itself protected the parked aircraft forward, it could badly damage the aircraft that ran into it. In prop-planes, the crew were fairly well protected, but in jets, with no propeller to protect them, the barrier wires could slice through the cockpit canopy and decapitate the crew. So, a safer and more efficient system was badly needed.

Save for the introduction of the crash barrier, flight-deck geometry had remained unchanged since the 1920s. The first attempt to develop an alternative came in the late 1940s, with the flexible flight deck. While the first jets were being developed, it was found that a streamlined form helped to increase the performance of the aircraft. Although it sounded far fetched,

Before the advent of the angled flight deck, crash barriers were raised to snag landing aircraft which missed the arrester wires. Here, a Sea Fury has been stopped by the barrier, but her propeller and cowling were damaged in the process.

it was proposed that naval jets would be built without undercarriages. They would land on a rubber-covered flight deck and caught by their tail hook when it snagged onto an arrester wire. Take-off was achieved by means of a trolley-mount on the catapult. Tests were carried out, and in 1948, after *Warrior* was fitted with a flexible flight deck, the first trials began. These used the Sea Vampire, and while they proved successful, the whole idea was quietly shelved, as any aerodynamic improvements were countered by the cost.

B

HMS *VICTORIOUS*, 1961

The Illustrious-class fleet carrier *Victorious* was a veteran of World War II, when her aircraft saw action against the *Bismarck*, launched strikes against the Italian battle fleet at Matapan and survived kamikaze attacks in the Pacific. By the late 1940s though, it was clear that if she was to remain a useful asset into the jet age, then she needed a major overhaul. So, from 1950 to 1958 she was essentially rebuilt from the hangar deck up. She emerged as the Royal Navy's most up-to-date carrier, with an angled flight deck, steam catapults, a mirror landing sight and some of the most advanced radar-systems in the world. Her embarked aircraft reflected her state-of-the-art look, as her wartime propeller-driven planes had been replaced by modern jets and helicopters. She also carried airborne early warning (AEW) aircraft, designed to extend her combat range by hundreds of miles. *Victorious* remained in service until 1967, a potent military asset during both the post-colonial era and the Cold War, and a symbol of the fading might of the post-war Royal Navy. This cutaway view shows her in July 1961, when she was deployed in the western end of the Persian Gulf. Her aircraft flew defensive sorties over Kuwait, helping to defuse the threat of an invasion of the small oil-rich British ally by neighbouring Iraq.

KEY

1. Port BS4 steam catapult
2. Axial deck centreline
3. Starboard BS4 steam catapult
4. Catapult control position
5. Supermarine scimitar (803 NAS)
6. Admiral's bridge
7. Ship's bridge
8. Type 974 surface search radar
9. Flying control position
10. Type 984 3-D air search radar
11. Forward aircraft lift
12. Mainmast with additional sensors
13. Jet blast deflector (one of two)
14. Aircraft crane
15. Westland whirlwind (825 NAS)
16. Angled flight deck centreline
17. After aircraft Lift

18. US 3-in. Mark 33 gun in twin mount (one of six mounts)
19. Propeller and shaft (one of three: port, centre and starboard)
20. Fairey Gannet AEW (849B NAS)
21. Boat deck
22. Transmitting mast (one of four)
23. Mirror landing sight DLPS Mk III (one of two)
24. Arrester wire (one of five)
25. Pop-up nylon emergency barrier
26. Engine room (one of three: port, centre and starboard)
27. Aircraft hanger
28. Boiler room (one of three: port, centre and starboard)
29. Pump system for steam catapults
30. Steam capstan and cable deck

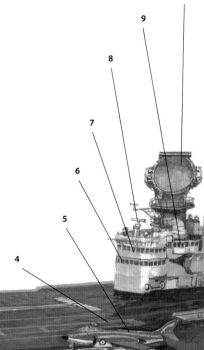
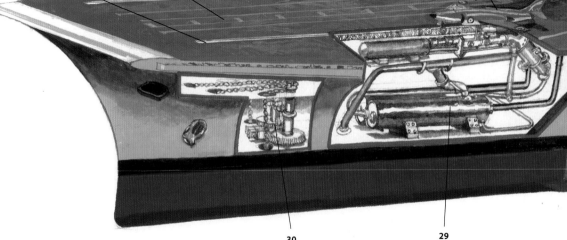

HMS *Victorious* (R38), 1961 specifications

Illustrious-class fleet carrier (sister ships: *Illustrious* and *Invincible*, both scrapped 1953–56)

Builder	Vickers-Armstrong, Tyneside
Launched and first commissioned	1937; 1941
Rebuilt	Portsmouth dockyard, 1950–58
Re-commissioned	January 1958
Decommissioned	March 1968
Scrapped	1969
Displacement	35,500 tons (fully laden)
Dimensions	length: 778ft 3in. overall (237.21m), beam: 95ft 9in. at waterline (29.18m), draught: 31ft fully-laden (9.45m)
Propulsion	three shafts, three Parsons geared turbines, six Admiralty three-drum boilers, generating 110,000 shp, endurance: 11,000 miles at 12 knots
Maximum speed	31 knots; fuel oil capacity; 4,180 tons
Armament	12 US 3in. Mark 33 guns in six twin mounts (three on each beam)
Sensors	type 984 3D air search radar, type 974 surface search radar, type 293Q target tracking radar, type 957 air beacon system
Protection	4.5in. belt, 3.5in. flight deck and hangar sides, 2.5in. hangar deck
Complement	2,400
Aircraft facilities	flight deck length: 775ft (236.22m), angled-deck of 8 ½°, two BS4 steam catapults (50,000lb launch capacity at 97kts), two mirror landing aids, five arrester wires, plus nylon emergency barriers
Hangar and lifts	412ft (125.58m), long hangar served by two lifts (both 42,000lb capacity)
Aircraft capacity	up to 36 aircraft, depending on type
Aviation fuel stocks	327,800 gallons AVCAT
Embarked aircraft, July 1961	803 NAS (Scimitars), 892 NAS (Sea Vixens), 849B NAS (Gannet AEWs), 825 NAS (Whirlwind helicopters)

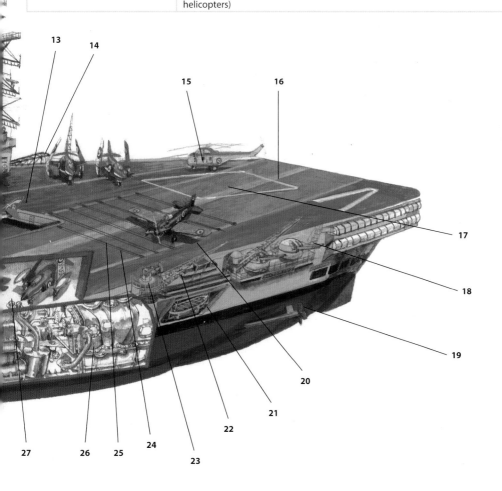

A Phantom FG-2 of 892 NAS landing on the deck of *Ark Royal*, c.1971, during a working up period off the Scottish coast. Note the snagged arrester wire, the projector landing sight on her port side, and the SAR helicopter off the carrier's port beam, in this case a Wessex 3.

The Westland Wyvern entered service in 1953, and served with eight FAA squadrons before being replaced four years later. Although designed as a torpedo plane, the Wyvern could also be used as fighter-bomber, armed with three 1,000lb bombs.

The real breakthrough to flight deck design came in mid-1951. During continued discussions about flexible flight decks, Capt Dennis Campbell, a naval representative at the Ministry of Aviation, sketched out a new flight deck configuration in which the flexible after deck was angled slightly to port. This meant that aircraft without undercarriages could land without the risk of hitting or bouncing over the crash barrier. Three weeks later, Lewis Boddington of the Royal Aircraft Establishment proposed that this angled flight deck be fitted to *Ark Royal*, which was then nearing completion. The Admiralty agreed to test the notion on *Triumph*; its axial flight deck was repainted in early 1952 to conform to Campbell's angled flight deck.

The whole idea of angling it over the side of the carrier was that if a landing was problematic, and the arrester hook didn't snag the aircraft, then the pilot could make a 'touch and go' landing. In other words, the pilot had to make his landing approach at the slowest possible safe flying speed. So, if he failed to arrest, then he could rev his engines again and fly off the edge of the flight deck, before 'going round again' and making another approach. This meant that air operations could continue largely uninterrupted by accidents involving the crash barrier, and without risking any parked aircraft. The trials proved a huge success, as did a similar evaluation on board the US Navy's carrier *Midway*. Although the trials on *Triumph* were very favourable, the Admiralty decided to delay its adoption of the angled flight deck until *Ark Royal* entered service. However, when the US Navy readily embraced the idea, it felt it had to follow its lead. So, in 1953, during a refit, the light carrier *Centaur* was duly fitted with an angled flight deck installed.

It was not until early 1955 that *Ark Royal* was commissioned, becoming the first aircraft carrier in the world to enter service with an angled flight deck installed. However, this deck was angled at only 5½° from the carrier's axis, making it less pronounced than Campbell and Boddington had intended. *Ark Royal*'s sister ship, *Eagle*, which had joined the fleet in late 1951, had an axial flight deck. This was rectified in the 1954–55 refit, when *Ark Royal* was also fitted with a 5½° angled flight deck. This was increased to 8½° during the major 1959–64 refit, thanks to lobbying by Cdr Eric 'Winkle' Brown, the Navy's foremost test pilot. *Victorious* also gained an 8° angled flight deck during her 1950–58 refit. However, the US Navy favoured a more pronounced angle of 10½°, in line with Campbell and Boddington's original idea. Appropriately enough, when *Ark Royal* entered service, Capt Campbell was her first commanding officer.

The adoption of the angled flight deck solved two problems. First it made carrier flying operations much safer, as it removed the need for a crash barrier. Although necessary to protect parked aircraft, the barrier was dangerous for the crew of the aircraft that became entangled in it. Inevitably it also meant damage to the aircraft. Even the introduction of a new nylon webbing barrier in 1952 didn't solve the problem, as it still needed a taut steel wire behind it. It reduced the chances of death or damage, but didn't eliminate them. With the introduction of the angled flight deck, if any problems arose while landing, the pilot could simply 'touch and go', and try again. As a result, the Fleet Air Arm's safety record improved remarkably. A nylon barrier, however, could still be rigged if required, if circumstances demanded it, such as in the case of an emergency landing.

Mirror landing aids

During the late 1940s, the accident rate on flight decks was alarmingly high, with 2 per cent ending badly. This was due in part to the high-performance, piston-engined planes in service, and the tendency of tail-wheeled aircraft to bounce when touching down. A new Standard Deck Landing Technique was introduced in 1949 to standardize the method used on both British and American carriers, but this too caused problems, as it meant a complete reversal of signals by the Deck Landing Control Officer (DLCO), which took some getting used to. However, practice helped, as did the fitting of dampeners to the aircraft's arrester hook. The experience of pilots and deck landing teams improved, particularly given the extensive flying operations conducted during the Korean War. By 1951, the accident rate had halved. Still, deck landing in powerful propeller-driven aircraft remained a risky business.

In theory, the arrival of even faster jet aircraft would have increased the risk of flight deck accidents. However, the adoption of the tricycle undercarriage improved the view of the pilot when landing, as he could see the flight deck throughout the whole approach and landing. The high speeds of jets meant that landings were still tricky, as the pilot and the DLCO had less time to correct any errors during the approach. This was particularly true when the carrier was pitching or rolling in a heavy sea. During the early 1950s, a naval test pilot, Cdr Nick Goodhart, realized that the real problem was one of pilot awareness. The DLCO with his bats could help, waving the pilot down, as could the experimental DLCO's semaphore system installed in *Victorious*, but Goodhart's solution was

While angled flight decks for landing-on and mirror landing sights greatly improved the safety of carrier operation, accidents still happened. Here a Buccaneer S1 caught its arrester wire, but then veered towards the port side of the flight deck. The wire saved her pilot and observer from being lost over the side. If that happened, the ever-present SAR helicopter would be hovering over the downed aircraft within half a minute.

A Sea Vixen of 890 NAS making her final approach to *Ark Royal* during a deployment in the Far East, 1965–66. Note that she isn't approaching directly astern of the carrier, but along the centreline of her angled flight deck. Note the SAR Wessex 1 helicopter off the carrier's port side.

far more effective. He proposed using a mirror as a landing aid. With a mirror, he could gauge his approach, and respond to any pitching or rolling of the flight deck.

By watching a mirror image of his aircraft as it landed, the pilot could make any last-minute corrections himself. Goodhart's mirror landing aid was installed facing aft on the after port side of the flight deck. A spare was usually carried on the starboard side. It was gyroscopically stabilized as well, to compensate for the movement of the ship. A white light (known as the 'meatball') at the end of the flight deck shone onto the centre of the concave mirror, and a row of green lights on either side of the mirror gave the pilot a reference plane. During his approach, the pilot could see if he was too high or too low, and adjust his approach accordingly. The mirror was slightly concave so that the pilot could still see it as he turned to make his approach onto an angled flight deck. If he was lined up on the flight deck centreline correctly, and was at the right speed and altitude, then the chances of a faulty landing were minimal.

It was a simple system, but it was also extremely effective. As a result, the accident rate soon dropped to just 0.5 per cent. The mirror landing system was tested aboard *Illustrious* and *Indomitable*, before being officially adopted in 1954, when it was installed in the light carrier *Albion*. During the next decade the original mirror landing sight was eventually adapted to produce the projector sight, which was easier to use in bad weather. Essentially, it did away with the mirror, and instead used graduated bars of light. These were first fitted to *Ark Royal* during her 1958–59 refit. Another modification was the addition of 'wave off' lights, controlled by the DLCO, if he felt the pilot had to abort the landing. The US Navy adopted Goodhart's system in 1955, and it soon became standard equipment aboard the world's carriers. It is still in use today, albeit in the much-modified device called the Optical Landing System (OLS), and relies on Fresnel lenses, similar to those used in lighthouses.

C — MODERNIZED CARRIERS *EAGLE* (1969) AND *ARK ROYAL* (1976)

1. *Eagle* (R05). In 1942, the first of three Audacious-class fleet carriers were laid down. These were planned as the next generation of British carrier but, in the end, only two were built. *Eagle*, the first of these, entered service in 1951, by which time she was already outdated. She was largely rebuilt, and re-emerged in 1964 as a carrier capable of handling modern jets such as the Buccaneer of 800 NAS, shown here **(1a)**. However, she only remained in operation for eight years, being decommissioned in 1972. This illustration shows *Eagle* in her heyday in 1969 when she took part in a succession of large-scale NATO exercises in the Mediterranean.

2. *Ark Royal* (R09). The Audacious-class carrier *Ark Royal* would be the Royal Navy's last conventional aircraft carrier, launching her aircraft using steam catapults. More positively, when she was commissioned in early 1955, she became the world's first carrier to enter service with an angled flight deck. This, together with a series of upgrades during refits, meant she remained an important naval asset for almost a quarter of a century. Although she never saw action, she contributed to NATO's naval force during the Cold War, and was deployed to help deter conflict with her aircraft flying patrols over British Honduras (now Belize) in 1972 when the Crown Colony was threatened with invasion. She was finally decommissioned in early 1979. This illustration shows her in 1977, when the author, then a schoolboy, watched her air operations from an accompanying destroyer. Also shown is a Royal Navy Phantom FG1 of 892 NAS **(2a)**. *Ark Royal* was the only British carrier capable of operating these powerful fighter bombers.

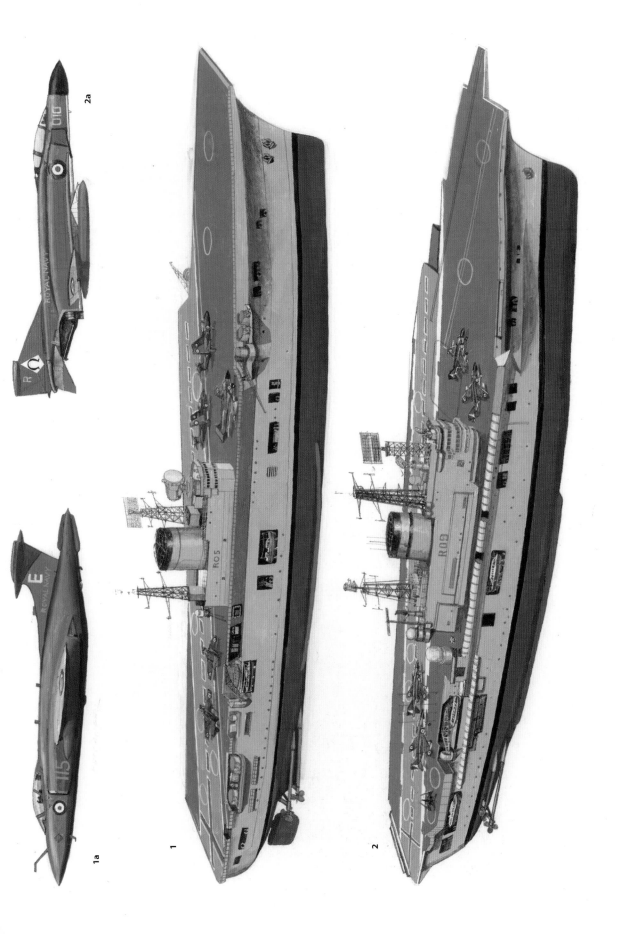

During the late 1940s and early 1950s, *Illustrious* became the testbed for a range of aircraft, either prototypes, land-based ones modified for naval use and others which had already been accepted by the Navy, but needed thorough evaluation before being deployed operationally. New ordnance or weaponry was also evaluated on the trials carrier, as depicted here by a ship's cartoonist.

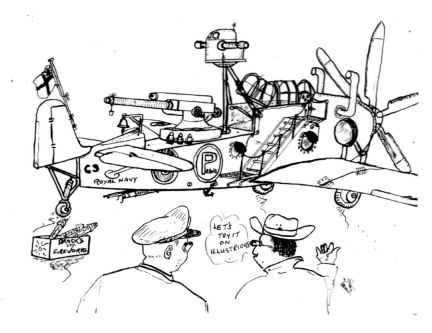

A trials version of the Supermarine Attacker F1, taking off from *Illustrious* with the assistance of RATOG, c.1947. The 'Rocket Assisted Take-Off Gear' was essentially a group of small rockets, attached to the rear of a heavy or overloaded aircraft to boost its speed during take-off. The RATOG system was widely used during the Korean War, but was rendered superfluous following the introduction of the steam catapult.

V/STOL aircraft

During the 1950s, the three major British contributions to post-war naval aviation – the steam catapult, the angled flight deck and the mirror landing sight – were all adopted by the US Navy, and so played a key role in the impressive development of the United States' carrier strike force. However, in Britain, the value of a carrier strike force was never fully appreciated by successive governments, which either cancelled new design projects or chose not to replace the ageing carrier fleet. This, ultimately, led to the temporary end of fixed-wing aviation in the Royal Navy when *Ark Royal*, the last of the operational aircraft carriers, was retired from service in 1979. By then though, not only was a class of three new light carriers being built, but it was designed to use a revolutionary new type of aircraft.

Like the propeller-driven aircraft that preceded them, the majority of jets were designed to take off and land conventionally, either on carriers or on land-based airfields. During the late 1940s, the US Navy began exploring the concept of Vertical/Short Take-Off and Landing (V/STOL) aircraft. These were jets that had no need for long runways, but could either become airborne after a short take-off run, or could take off and land vertically. At the time, their development never got any further than the prototype stage. However, the British aircraft manufacturer Hawker-Siddeley resurrected the idea in the late 1950s, and began developing its own V/STOL design. Its prototype, the P.1127, made its first flight in 1960. After a few more modifications, the P.1127, dubbed the Kestrel, conducted trials aboard *Ark Royal* in early 1963. At that point though, the Navy wasn't especially interested in the V/STOL concept.

This would change in 1967 after the RAF ordered an operational version of the aircraft. By then, it was known as the Harrier. The US, Spanish and Indian navies all evaluated the Harrier, and in 1971 it was adopted by the US Marine Corps, which designated it the AV-8A Harrier. By then, the Royal Navy was facing the loss of all its remaining carriers, save for the three Illustrious-class light carriers, which had been designed to fulfil an anti-submarine warfare (ASW) role. Essentially, these would be helicopter carriers. However, the Royal Navy developed an alternative use for them as 'through-deck cruisers'. Although these would be too small to operate conventional jets, they might be suitable for V/STOL ones.

A Sea Harrier FRS2 of 801 NAS ranged on the deck of the light carrier *Ark Royal* during the late 1980s, together with two of its flight deck crew. The trolley attached to the aircraft's front wheel is used to move the jet into position, ready for take-off.

Fortuitously, in 1972, Hawker-Siddeley, now part of British Aerospace (BAe), developed a naval strike fighter variant of its 'jump jet' – the Sea Harrier.

The Royal Navy purchased its first Sea Harriers in 1975, and when *Invincible* entered service in 1980, the Sea Harriers formed part of its air wing, together with the Sea King ASW helicopter. This light carrier, and her sister ships which followed, had a dual role. They could perform their ASW function, fulfilling the Royal Navy's NATO commitment in the North Atlantic. The Sea Harrier though, also gave these ships the capability to conduct strike missions and to fly combat air patrol (CAP) missions to protect the fleet. A limitation though, with the Sea Harrier, was that it needed around 300m of runway to take off, which was longer than the flight deck of *Invincible*. The solution was the adoption of the ski jump ramp, which allowed the Sea Harrier to take off in roughly half the distance, even when fully laden with fuel and munitions.

The ski jump idea was first developed in the early 1960s by Lt.Cdr Doug Taylor of *Victorious*. During the Indonesian Confrontation (1963–66), he noted that in extremely hot conditions the steam catapult often failed to work, due to the expansion of the catapult runners. His solution was the 'runway in the sky', a ramp designed to allow jets to become airborne without the use of a catapult. Taylor had heard of the way a ramp had been used in 1944 to allow heavily laden aircraft to take off from the carrier *Furious*

The light carrier HMS *Hermes*, pictured off Gibraltar in early 1979. At the time she was taking part in a series of joint exercises with the USS *Dwight D. Eisenhower*, when their Sea Kings provided ASW protection for the task force. Incidentally the author was on board her at the time.

during air attacks on the German battleship *Tirpitz*. This idea developed into the ski jump ramp, which was fitted onto the forward end of the flight deck of the Invincible-class light carriers during their construction. The ramp allowed fully laden Sea Harriers to take off after a run of just 146 metres.

The last remaining light carrier, *Hermes*, was also refitted with a ski jump ramp during 1979–80. *Invincible* and *Illustrious* were fitted with 7° ramps, but after some re-evaluation, the last of the class, *Ark Royal*, received a 12° one, which worked more efficiently. Subsequently, her two earlier sister ships were refitted with the steeper ramp during refits. The ski jump ramp can really be considered the fourth great British contribution to post-war carrier design. While designed to turn the Sea Harrier into an effective carrier aircraft, it was generally seen as an ideal way to boost the take-off performance of any carrier-borne jet aircraft. As such, it is seen as a viable alternative to the steam catapult, and has been fitted to Britain's new generation of Queen Elizabeth-class carriers.

The carrier's evolving role

The coming of peace in September 1945 led to a re-evaluation of the Royal Navy's purpose and the role of its sizeable carrier fleet. For a while, the carriers of the British Pacific Fleet were kept busy, ensuring the surrender of the remaining Japanese outposts, repatriating prisoners of war and bringing home military personnel. By then though, Winston Churchill had already delivered his Iron Curtain speech, and it was clear that Britain's most likely adversary in any major war would be the Soviet Union. That said, it was also a traumatic period for Britain as its global empire was dismantled, and a looser Commonwealth was created in its stead. It was also a period of significant post-war austerity in Britain, as the government tried to pay off its wartime debts. This in turn led to the rapid scaling back of the carrier fleet and a reappraisal of its strategic purpose.

Essentially, the carrier fleet had three roles. The first was a reiteration of Britain's old role as a global policeman, protecting British interests overseas and offering a means of supporting British military operations around the globe. So, carriers were deployed to international hot spots, where they were able to support British troops during a number of brushfire conflicts in places such as Greece, Palestine, Malaya, Borneo and Aden. Traditionally, the cruiser had been the preferred warship for this kind of mission, but it was found that the carrier was more effective and versatile in performing this gunboat diplomacy role. The two other roles involved a limited or full-scale proxy war with the Soviet Union and its allies. Primarily, this involved protecting Britain's sea lanes and exerting sea control. In the case of the Korean War, this also involved the support of UN military operations on land.

The foundation of NATO in 1949 led to the Royal Navy forming a key part of NATO's naval commitment in the North Atlantic. If war erupted, carriers deployed

An impromptu carrier strike force made up of *Eagle* (left) and *Ark Royal* (right), pictured from the Rock of Gibraltar in October 1965. They weren't deployed together though – *Eagle* had just completed exercises with the US Sixth Fleet, and *Ark Royal* was on her way out to the Far East.

in the Arctic Ocean or Norwegian Sea would help protect NATO's northern flank, while supporting ASW operations against the Soviet Union's growing submarine fleet. This then, required a division of the Navy's carriers between overseas and home water deployment. Between 1947 and 1952 the Navy had two fleet carriers and four or five light carriers in operation, while three more fleet carriers fulfilled training roles and were capable of being redeployed in time of war. By 1959, the carrier strike force had been reduced to just five carriers (three fleet and two light carriers). This meant that at any one time, one fleet carrier and one light carrier could be deployed overseas, with a similar deployment in home waters.

In 1956, the carrier strike force saw action during the Suez Crisis, in which *Eagle* was supported by the light carriers *Albion* and *Bulwark*. *Ocean* and *Theseus* were also involved in the crisis, albeit as hastily converted commando carriers, which were equipped with helicopters. These proved so valuable during the Suez Crisis that afterwards, *Albion* and *Bulwark* were also converted into commando carriers when *Ocean* and *Theseus* were withdrawn from operational service. By the late 1960s, the Royal Navy's ageing handful of remaining carriers had less than a decade of operational life left in them. The Royal Navy pinned its hopes on the CVA-01 project to reinvigorate its carrier strike force. So, when this project was axed in 1966, it was clear that the lifespan of the carrier fleet was limited.

During this period, British carriers were still involved in overseas conflicts, the most significant being the Indonesian Confrontation (1963–66), but a steady reduction in overseas possessions meant that there was less need for a permanent overseas presence. Instead, it was the Royal Navy's NATO commitment which would increasingly occupy the carrier fleet during its final years. However, this largely meant ASW operations, which in turn required helicopters rather than fixed-wing aircraft. By 1973, only *Ark Royal* was left, by which time her primary role was to provide air protection for the rest of the fleet and to provide an air strike capability in time of war. Her demise in 1979 was followed, after a brief hiatus, by the arrival of *Invincible*, whose Sea Harriers were expected to fulfil the same double role.

HMS *Eagle*, with Wyverns ranged on her after deck, leads a NATO carrier strike force into the Trondheimfjord in late September 1953, after completing Operation *Mariner*, a major NATO exercise in the North Atlantic. The two carriers astern of her are of the Colossus class, one of them being the French *Arromanches*.

A Hawker Sea Vixen of 890 NAS, landing on *Ark Royal* in 1966, while the carrier was operating with the Far Eastern Fleet. During this period the carrier took part in the Beira Patrol, when the radar on 890 NAS's Sea Vixens proved ideal at locating and then identifying suspicious vessels in the Mozambique Channel.

A Supermarine Seafire burning after a serious crash on the deck of *Implacable*, 1948. During this period there were numerous flight deck 'incidents' involving this graceful but fragile fighter. This was particularly true on *Implacable* and *Illustrious*, as both were used as training carriers. This naval version of the Spitfire was a beautiful aircraft to fly, but not nearly robust enough for carrier operations.

In some ways the Falklands War represented a brief return to the days of an overseas carrier strike force. In early April 1982, when the British Task Force sailed for the South Atlantic, the Carrier Battle Group was at its core. Between them, *Hermes* and *Invincible* had 31 Sea Harriers embarked, as well as 15 Sea King ASW helicopters. Their task was to perform CAP missions to protect the Task Force, but also to carry out strike missions against ground targets in the Falklands. Their success in these roles helped underline the need for a carrier group in the Royal Navy, which helped to ensure another two decades of jet aviation in the Fleet Air Arm. This in turn demonstrated the continued value of carriers in terms of power projection, particularly after the end of the Cold War, when Britain became involved in a number of overseas conflicts that required a naval presence.

While this strategic flexibility was lost when the Sea Harrier was retired from service, the legacy of the Falklands was that the need for this type of global power projection was self-evident. So, even when *Illustrious*, the last of Britain's post-war carriers, was decommissioned, the first of two new British super carriers was nearing completion in Rosyth in Scotland.

This means that after a short gap, the Royal Navy, at the time of writing, once again has a carrier strike force worthy of the name. The Fleet Air Arm too, is now back in the fixed-wing aviation business, as the two Queen Elizabeth-class carriers embark the F-35 Lightning II multi-role combat aircraft, as well as helicopters as a Maritime Protection Package, a term which covers AEW and ASW capabilities. It is expected that these two carriers will remain in service until at least the middle of the 21st Century. Their future role and their aircraft requirements are hard to predict, despite the resurgence of Russia, Britain's old Cold War adversary.

One thing that the story of Britain's post-war carriers has taught us is that the age of the ship is less important than the ability to upgrade it, in line with the latest technological developments, and to adapt its role to reflect

D

LIGHT CARRIERS: *ALBION* (1956) AND *CENTAUR* (1960)

1. HMS *Albion* (R07). The second of the Centaur-class light carriers to enter service, *Albion* was commissioned in 1954, and for the next two years, served with the Mediterranean, Home and Far Eastern fleets. In late 1956 a refit in Portsmouth was called short due to the looming Suez Crisis, and in November, she joined the joint Anglo-French carrier strike force assembled in the Eastern Mediterranean. During the week-long Operation *Musketeer*, her air group bombed Egyptian airfields and provided air cover during Allied amphibious and airborne assaults near Port Said. She was subsequently converted into a commando carrier and remained in service until 1972. This illustration shows the carrier as she appeared during Operation *Musketeer*, together with one of the embarked **(1a)** Sea Hawks (800 NAS) which took part in attacks on Al Naza airfield outside Cairo.

2. HMS *Centaur* (R39, then R06). In 1953 *Centaur* was commissioned with an axial deck, but was then fitted with a partial (5 ½°) angled flight deck. After two years serving with the Mediterranean and Home fleets, she was refitted with steam catapults, enabling her to carry the Sea Venom. *Centaur* was recommissioned in 1958 and deployed in the Indian Ocean and Far East until 1962. She was re-fitted again in 1963 and given a Type 965 radar on a lattice mast, then headed 'East of Suez' until late 1964. She was finally paid off the following September. This illustration shows *Centaur* in 1960 when her embarked air group engaged in anti-piracy operations off Aden. The aircraft **(2a)** is a Sea Venom of 891 NAS.

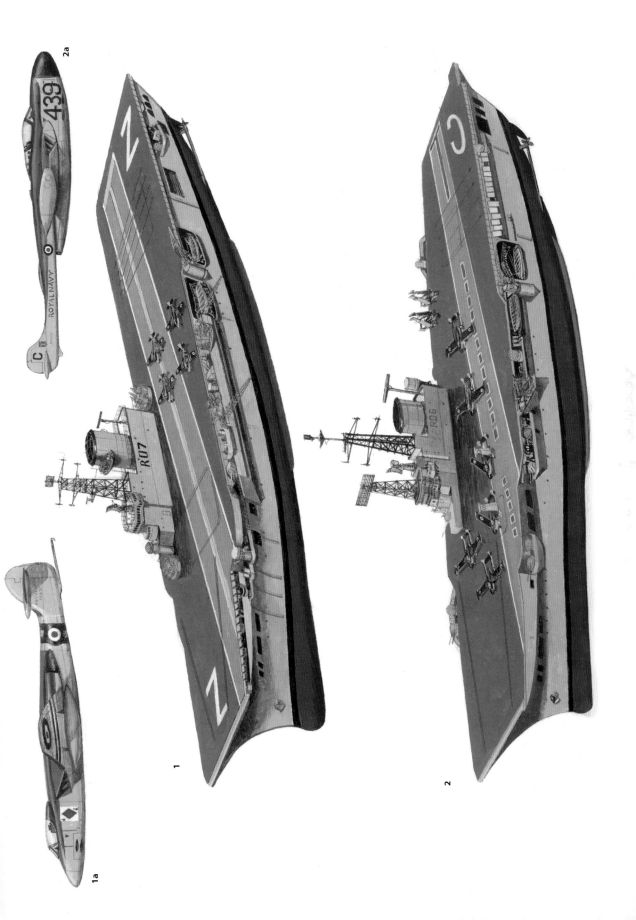

2a

439

ROYAL NAVY

C

1

1a

2

new needs. This is how *Victorious*, a fleet carrier that flew strikes against the *Bismarck* in 1941, was still able to operate powerful jet-powered strike aircraft, such as the Buccaneer, over a quarter of a century later. It is also how the Centaur-class light carrier *Hermes* went through several guises, emerging as the flagship of the British Task Force during the Falklands War, before seeing another three decades of service with the Indian Navy. When she was finally decommissioned in 2017, she was the oldest operational aircraft carrier in the world. If the two Queen Elizabeths can emulate their post-war forebears, then the future of British naval aviation looks more promising than it has at any point since 1945.

Aircraft

At the end of World War II, the Fleet Air Arm still operated a number of British-built aircraft such as the Fairey Barracuda torpedo bomber, the Fairey Firefly and the Supermarine Seafire fighter, the naval version of the Spitfire. The versatile Firefly was described as the best British naval aircraft of the war, combining fighter, reconnaissance and strike roles. However, an increasing number of American-built Grumman Avenger torpedo bombers and Vought Corsair fighters emerged, which were usually larger and more robust than their British counterparts.

Examples of embarked aircraft, 1945	
Victorious	*Formidable*
849 Sqn (Avengers)	848 Sqn (Avengers)
1834 and 1836 Sqns (Corsairs)	1841 and 1842 Sqns (Corsairs)
Indefatigable	*Venerable*
820 Sqn (Avengers)	814 Sqn (Barracudas)
887 and 894 Sqns (Seafires)	1851 Sqn (Corsairs)
1770 and 1772 Sqns (Fireflies)	

A Grumman Avenger III, a Lend-Lease aircraft which was designed as a torpedo bomber, but could equally serve as a bomber or reconnaissance aircraft. After the war, most of these aircraft were either returned to the United States or ditched over the side. In 1953 a modified version of this aircraft without the after turret was reintroduced into service as an ASW aircraft, before being phased out in 1960.

After the war, most American-built Lend-Lease aircraft were either returned to the United States or disposed of, to avoid paying for them. Disposal involved pushing them over the side of the carrier. A number though, were retained in service, including the Avenger ASW version and the new Douglas Skyraider AEW aircraft. By the start of the Korean War in 1950, the remaining carriers of the strike fleet embarked Seafires, Sea Furies and Fireflies. These propeller-driven planes proved effective in combat air patrols and ground strike missions during the Korean conflict.

However, a number of Blackburn Firebrand torpedo planes were also embarked in carriers in home waters, despite the plane's unpopularity with pilots. This was due to the cockpit being set some 15ft behind the engine, making it hard to see the deck when landing. The Supermarine Sea

Otter float planes, successors to the Walruses, were also embarked as plane guards – standing by to rescue downed aircrew in the event of a ditching.

Examples of embarked aircraft operating off Korea, 1950–53	
Triumph (1950)	*Glory* (1951)
800 Sqn (Seafires)	804 Sqn (Sea Furies)
827 Sqn (Fireflies)	821 Sqn (Fireflies)
Theseus (1951)	*Ocean* (1952)
807 Sqn (Sea Furies)	802 Sqn (Sea Furies)
810 Sqn (Fireflies)	810 Sqn (Fireflies)

However, the Seafire was not particularly robust, and despite performing well in the air, it was vulnerable to damage when landing. The Firefly was retained in service until 1956. A more robust, piston-engined alternative to the Seafire was the Hawker Sea Fury, beloved by pilots, and viewed as the fleet's ultimate piston-engined fighter. The De Havilland Sea Hornet, a newly introduced naval version of the Mosquito, was also well liked, and the Royal Navy's test pilot, Lt.Cdr 'Winkle' Brown described it as a superb aircraft. There were two versions, a single-seater and a two-seater night fighter. Another new, prop-driven aircraft to enter service during the early 1950s was the Westland Wyvern, a strike aircraft, which saw action during the Suez Crisis (1956). Unusually for a prop-plane, it was fitted with ejector seats, and when two were shot down over Egypt the pilots ejected safely.

These propeller-driven planes were soon to be replaced by the jet. For the Royal Navy, the jet age officially began in December 1945 when 'Winkle' Brown landed a prototype twin-engined De Havilland Vampire on the flight deck of *Ocean*. This, the world's first carrier landing by a jet, was a success, but the aircraft didn't lend itself to naval use, and so was only deployed in a limited, evaluative way. Instead, it would be the Supermarine Attacker that would be the first jet fighter to be embarked operationally by the Fleet Air Arm. A prototype was flown in 1947, and the production version became operational at sea in 1952. It was soon superseded by the much sleeker Hawker Sea Hawk in 1954. This elegant jet became the Navy's primary fighter aircraft for the rest of the decade.

Carrier aircraft operating off Suez, 1956		
Eagle	*Albion*	*Bulwark*
830 and 831 Sqns (Wyverns)	800, 802 and 810 Sqns (Sea Hawks)	804 and 897 Sqns (Sea Hawks)
891 and 893 Sqns (Sea Venoms)	809, 894 and 895 Sqns (Sea Venoms)	
849A Sqn (Skyraiders)	849B Sqn (Skyraiders)	
849D Sqn (Gannet AEW)		

Its companion was the De Havilland Sea Venom, a two-seater fighter, which filled the need for a larger fighter. A prototype was flown in 1951, and it entered frontline service in 1956. It replaced the prop-driven Sea Hornet, and was embarked in *Albion* and *Eagle* in time to see action over Suez. Later, an electronic, counter-measured (ECM) version was produced. Both the Vampire and the Sea Venom had a twin-boom tail arrangement, giving them a striking appearance. The Royal Navy primarily used the Sea Venom as an interceptor, but it lacked the speed it really needed for the job. Fortunately for the Fleet Air Arm, De Havilland had already begun design work on the Sea Vixen, a jet capable of supersonic speed. This development suffered a major setback in 1952 when a prototype, the DH-110 disintegrated in mid-air at the Farnborough Air Show, killing 31 people, the crew of two and 29 on the ground.

The problem was traced to the faulty design of the wings, which had been subjected to the stresses of supersonic speed. This was rectified, and work continued. In 1955 the Fleet Air Arm ordered a naval version of the jet, and the following year a naval prototype landed on *Ark Royal*. The result, the Sea Vixen, entered service in 1959. This was a truly modern jet fighter, capable of high speed, and equipped with both radar and air-to-air missiles. Its strange, asymmetric cockpit layout did little to reduce the beauty of this elegant two-seater aircraft. It remained in service throughout the 1960s, its longevity helped by its ability to land on the fleet's smaller axial carriers.

Examples of embarked aircraft, 1960–70	
Hermes (1960)	*Victorious (1963)*
804 Sqn (Scimitars)	801 Sqn (Buccaneers)
890 Sqn (Sea Vixens)	893 Sqn (Sea Vixens)
814 Sqn (Wessex)	814 Sqn (Wessex)
849A Sqn (Gannet AEW)	849A Sqn (Gannet AEW)
Eagle (1964)	*Ark Royal (1964)*
800 Sqn (Buccaneers)	803 Sqn (Scimitars)
800B Sqn (Scimitars)	890 Sqn (Sea Vixens)
899 Sqn (Sea Vixens)	929 Sqn (Wessex)
820 Sqn (Wessex)	849C Sqn (Gannet AEW)
849B Sqn (Gannet AEW)	
Plus 1 COD Gannet	

During this period, a small number of American aircraft, the Grumman Avenger AS5 and the Douglas Skyraider, were purchased for anti-submarine and airborne early warning roles respectively. Each tended to be embarked in flights rather than squadrons, denoted by a flight letter (for example, 849A for A Flight of 849 Sqn's Skyraiders embarked in *Eagle*, which provided air warning cover over Suez). In 1955, the Avenger was replaced by the Fairey Gannet, an ungainly aircraft with two contra-rotating propellers. In 1959, an AEW version replaced the Skyraider. By then though, the ASW version of the Gannet had been dropped, as it was found that helicopters could do the job more efficiently. Helicopters had proved their worth in Korea, and the Fleet Air Arm quickly recognized their potential.

The first of these, the Westland Dragonfly, was used as an SAR plane-guard, flying just off the carrier, ready to rescue the crew if an aircraft was forced to ditch. It was soon replaced by the Westland Whirlwind, a British,

licence-built version of the Sikorsky Chikasaw. It proved ideal for ASW operations, despite some teething problems. These were overcome in an improved British helicopter, the Wessex HAS1, which first saw operational service in 1961. Later in the decade, an improved ASW version, the Wessex HAS3 entered service, and would remain in use until the early 1980s. A commando-carrying version, the Wessex HAS5 was also produced, and embarked in the Royal Navy's commando carriers. Finally, the Westland Sea King, introduced in 1969, replaced the Wessex 3 as an ASW helicopter, and was subsequently adapted as an AEW replacement for the Gannet. The Sea King remained in Fleet Air Arm service until 2011.

By 1958, the third generation of carrier jet aircraft had entered service. With its trans-sonic performance generating speeds of over 600mph, the Supermarine Scimitar was the most powerful jet in the Fleet Air Arm. It was also the largest and heaviest, which made it something of a liability in the fleet's smaller carriers. Accident rates were high, particularly on carriers without angled flight decks. However, as a strike fighter, it represented a real step forward, and it could outperform any other naval jet of its day. It was to be replaced by the even more impressive Blackburn Buccaneer. The Buccaneer was a real thoroughbred, designed primarily for low-level below-the-radar flying. It entered service in 1962, but it was soon found that this first version was underpowered. This prompted an improved Buccaneer S2 version, powered by Rolls-Royce Spey engines. The Buccaneer remained in service until the decommissioning of *Ark Royal* in the late 1970s.

ABOVE LEFT
The unmistakably stumpy lines of the Skyraider I AEW, an American-built aircraft, and introduced into service with the Fleet Air Arm in 1952. This one is one of the four planes of A flight, 849 NAS, which was embarked on *Eagle* from 1955 until 1959.

ABOVE RIGHT
Blackburn Buccaneer S2s of 880 NAS displayed with their wings folded on the forward flight deck of *Eagle*, during the carrier's visit to Freemantle in Australia in early 1968. The S2 version of the Buccaneer was in service from 1965 to 1978.

Examples of embarked aircraft, 1969–78		
Eagle (1969)	Ark Royal (1970)	Hermes (1975)
800 Sqn (Buccaneers)	809 Sqn (Buccaneers)	845 Sqn (Wessex)
899 Sqn (Sea Vixens)	982 Sqn (Phantoms)	814 Sqn (Sea Kings)
826 Sqn (Wessex)	849B Sqn (Gannet AEW)	
849D Sqn (Gannet AEW)		

During the late 1950s, the McDonnell Aircraft Corporation in the USA designed a large supersonic interceptor, which could also be used as a fighter bomber. This was the Phantom F-4, which first entered service with the US Navy in 1961. This coincided with a period of upheaval in the declining British aviation industry, which saw the amalgamation of several famous companies into two, in order to stay competitive. The Royal Navy's attempts

The Invincible-class light carriers used a ski jump at the forward end of the flight deck to give the Sea Harrier the boost it needed to take off on a relatively short deck. Next to it is the pit for the carrier's Sea Dart SAM system, its primary defence against air attack.

to procure a replacement for the Sea Vixen were thwarted by political and financial problems, and so the Fleet Air Arm turned to McDonnell. As a result, it was agreed to build Phantoms in Britain under licence, powered by Rolls-Royce Spey engines. The result was the Phantom F-4K, which entered service in 1969.

However, these large, powerful jets needed blast-deflectors – water-cooled steel flaps which absorbed the afterburner exhaust when the Phantom took off. These were only fitted in *Ark Royal*, so it alone was capable of embarking the aircraft. During the 1970s, *Ark Royal* embarked both Phantoms and Buccaneers, but it was clear that the Fleet Air Arm's days of fixed-wing aviation were drawing to a close. As a result, the Phantom was withdrawn from Fleet Air Arm service in 1978, and the aircraft transferred to the RAF, which continued to operate the Phantom until 1989. By then though, the Fleet Air Arm had a new jet in service. The Sea Harrier, produced by British Aerospace (BAe), entered operational service in 1980–81, embarked in *Hermes* and *Invincible*.

Carrier battle group, Falklands War, 1982	
Hermes	*Invincible*
800 Sqn (Sea Harriers)	801 Sqn (Sea Harriers)
826 Sqn (Sea Kings)	820 Sqn (Sea Kings)
846 Sqn (Sea Kings – *commando*)	
Air Group reinforced by 809 and 899 Sqns (Sea Harriers), 1 Sqn RAF (Harriers) and 815 Sqn (Lynx) during the conflict.	

E **LIGHT CARRIERS *HERMES* AND *INVINCIBLE*, FALKLANDS WAR, 1982**

1. *Hermes* (R12). When she was finally decommissioned by the Indian Navy in 2020, the carrier *Viraat*, formerly the Centaur-class light carrier *Hermes*, was the oldest operational aircraft carrier in the world. Although she was first commissioned in 1959, *Hermes* had first been laid down during World War II. Until 1970 she was a conventional light carrier, built with an angled flight deck but was then refitted as a commando carrier, and her fixed-wing aircraft facilities were removed. *Hermes* was reconfigured again in 1976, becoming an ASW Carrier, embarking Sea King helicopters. In 1980–81 she was rebuilt again to carry the Sea Harrier **(1a)** which included the fitting of a 7 ½° 'ski ramp'. She served as the Task Force flagship during the Falklands War (1982), embarking 26 Sea Harriers and RAF Harriers, as well as Sea Kings. *Hermes* was placed in reserve in 1984, then sold to the Indian Navy.

2. *Invincible* (R05). *Invincible*, the namesake of her three-ship class, was laid down as a Light ASW carrier, but was converted to carry the Sea Harrier while still on the stocks. This modification involved the fitting of a 7° 'ski jump' ramp, to port of her Sea Dart SAM launcher. *Invincible* entered service in July 1980 and, together with *Hermes*, formed the Task Force Carrier Strike Group during the Falklands War (1982). Her planned air wing of eight Sea Harriers and ten Sea King ASW helicopters was expanded during the conflict. Lessons learned saw her refitted on her return with more close-range AA weapons including Phalanx, later replaced by Goalkeeper CIWS. In 1982, the British Government planned to sell *Invincible* to Australia but the plan was scuppered by the Argentinian invasion. Instead, she remained in service until 2010. Pictured with her is one of the embarked Sea Kings of 820 NAS **(2a)**, in the colour scheme used during the Falklands War.

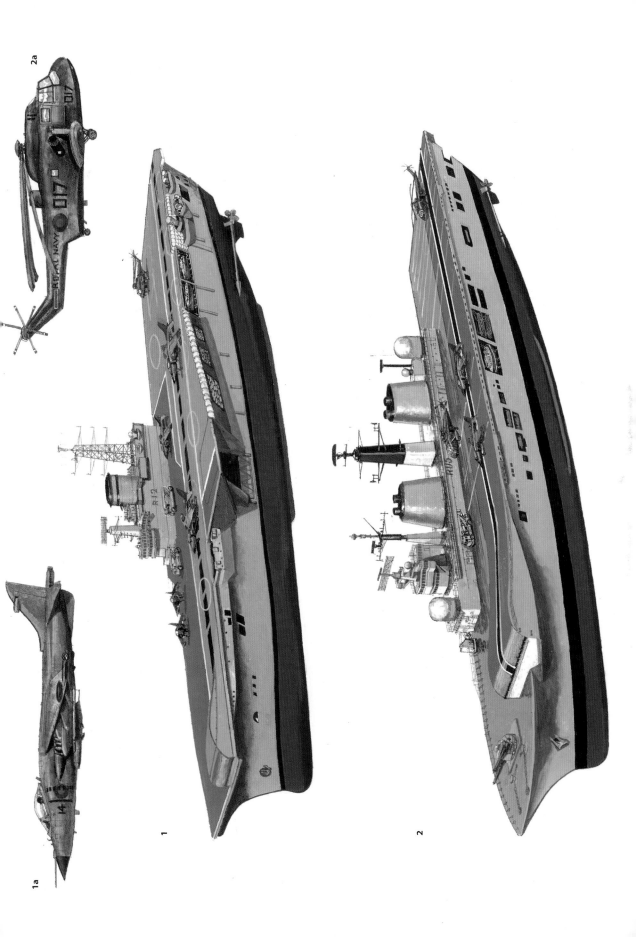

2a

1a

1

2

The aircraft was the result of decades of development by Hawker Siddeley into V/STOL aircraft – the first P.1127 prototype having landed on *Ark Royal* in 1963. The naval version was developed by BAe, after Hawker Siddeley was amalgamated into the company in 1977. The Sea Harrier might have been half the speed of the Phantom, with a fraction of its range and payload, but it did keep the Fleet Air Arm in the business of operating high-performance supersonic jet aircraft. It had its advantages too – it was comparatively small and light, which eased hangar storage problems, and the single-seat aircraft was extremely manoeuvrable. Its dog-fighting capabilities came to the fore during the Falklands War. Without the Sea Harrier, Britain would have been hard-pressed to win the war and liberate the archipelago. The retirement of the Sea Harrier in 2006 marked the end of an era for the Royal Navy. The end of fixed-wing aviation in the service – at least for a time – also brought the story of Britain's post-war carriers and their aircraft to a close. However, it hoped that the subsequent resurrection of both Royal Navy carriers and Fleet Air Arm jets means that a new age in British naval aviation will be as dramatic as that of the post-war era.

Fleet Air Arm aircraft, 1945–2010

Propeller-driven						
Aircraft	**Type**	**In service**	**Maximum speed**	**Weight**	**Endurance /Range (hours/miles)**	**Ordnance**
Sea Otter	SAR	1944–52	130kts	10,000lb	3.2 (630nm)	MG
Barracuda	Torpedo Bomber	1943–53	178kts	14,100lb	4 (977nm)	MG, T, B
Avenger		1943–46	225kts	16,400lb	5.8 (905nm)	T, B, R
Firebrand		1946–51	295kts	17,500lb	2.9 (643nm)	T, B, R
Corsair		1943–46	325kts	11,800lb	2.7 (1,005nm)	MG
Seafire	Fighter/Strike Fighter	1948–52	393kts	11,615lb	1.1 (817nm)	C, B, R
Sea Fury	Strike	1948–53	400kts	12,500lb	1.7 (904nm)	C, B, R
Sea Hornet		1948–57	374kts	18,250lb	3 (750nm)	C, B, R
Firefly	Strike	1948–55	330kts	16,096lb	6.5 (747nm)	C, B, R
Wyvern		1954–58	300kts	24,500lb	2.6 (1,025nm)	C, B, R, T
Avenger AS5		1953–55	227kts	16,761lb	4.3 (982nm)	B, R, DC
Gannet	ASW	1955–58	245kts	19,600lb	4.9 (575nm)	B, R, DC
Skyraider	AEW	1951–60	305kts	18,300lb	7.8 (868nm)	–
Gannet		1959–78	217kts	25,000lb	6 (700nm)	–

Jet-powered						
Aircraft	**Type**	**In service**	**Maximum speed**	**Weight**	**Endurance/Range (hours/miles)**	**Ordnance**
Sea Vampire		1949–56	457kts	12,660lb	2.35 (783nm)	C
Attacker		1951–54	513kts	11,500lb	1.4 (513nm)	C
Sea Hawk		1956–60	455kts	12,500lb	1 (490nm)	C, B, R
Scimitar	Fighter	1958–66	617kts	40,000lb	2.4 (1,500nm)	C, B, R, AAM
Sea Venom		1956–60	430kts	15,800lb	1.75 (500nm)	C, R
Sea Vixen		1964–72	550kts	37,000lb	2 (1,200nm)	B, R, AAM
Buccaneer	Strike	1961–78	625kts	45,000lb	1.5 (3,000nm)	B, R, ASM
Phantom	Fighter-bomber	1970–78	1,280kts	56,000lb	1 (1,000nm)	B, AAM
Sea Harrier		1980–2010	625kts	26,000lb	2.25 (250nm)	C, B, AAM

Helicopters							
Aircraft	Type	In service	Maximum speed	Weight	Endurance (hours)		Ordnance
Dragonfly	SAR	1950–60	89kts	5,871lb	2 (300nm)		–
Whirlwind		1957–60	60kts	7,800lb	3.8 (290nm)		T
Wessex I	ASW/SAR	1961–67	120kts	12,600lb	2.5 (340nm)		T
Wessex 3		1967–83	110kts	12,700lb	1.5 (300nm)		T, DC
Sea King		1969–2011	112kts	21,000lb	4.5 (664nm)		T, DC, NDB
Sea King	AEW	1982–2010	110kts	21,400lb	5 (420nm)		–

Note: If more than one version of the aircraft was in service, then the details given are those of the most commonly embarked variant.
Ordnance: AAM: Air-to-Air Missiles, ASM: Air-to-Ship Missile, B: Bombs, C: Cannons, DC: Depth Charges, MG: Machine Guns, NDB: Nuclear Depth Bomb, R: Rockets, T: Torpedo
Type: ASW: Anti-Submarine, AEW: Airborne Early Warning, SAR: Search and Rescue

CARRIERS IN ACTION

In the immediate aftermath of World War II, the carriers of the British Pacific Fleet were used to repatriate troops and prisoners of war, and to assist in the surrender of the last pockets of Japanese resistance. By then, the post-war cull of carriers was well under way, and by 1947 Britain's operational carrier strike force was reduced to just two fleet and five light carriers. Others, however, were used for training, or like *Illustrious*, serving as test beds for a new generation of naval aircraft. These carriers were deployed in the world's trouble spots as Britain oversaw the dismantling of the British Empire, and dealt with insurgency and unrest in Malaya and Palestine. Then, in June 1950, the Korean War erupted. As she was in the region, *Triumph* was quick to lend the weight of her embarked aircraft to assist the South Korean army. During the conflict, the aircraft of *Glory*, *Ocean*, *Theseus* and *Triumph* all flew numerous sorties over Korea.

Their aircraft were primarily employed in attacking ground targets, but on 9 August 1952 a Sea Fury from 802 Naval Air Squadron shot down a Mig-15. A flight of four Sea Furies was patrolling at 4,000ft over Chinnampo in North Korea when they were 'jumped by eight' of these Soviet-built jets. In the ensuing dogfight, a Sea Fury shot the faster Mig down when it overshot him. The rest of the Mig squadron broke off the action. Official credit for the 'kill' was given to Lt Peter 'Hoagy' Carmichael, but it was probably Sub-Lt Brian 'Smoo' Ellis who completed the action. It was the first time a propeller-driven fighter had shot down a jet in combat.

BELOW LEFT
Until 1952 the Royal Navy's standard search and rescue (SAR) aircraft was the Supermarine Sea Otter. It was replaced by the American-designed Dragonfly, a helicopter built under licence by Westland. These proved excellent in the SAR role, until their replacement by the Westland Whirlwind in 1954. This HR 1 version of 705 NAS was pictured in 1952, during SAR trials and evaluation on board *Illustrious*.

BELOW RIGHT
Aircraft handlers pushing a Hawker Sea Fury FB 11 strike aircraft up the flight deck of a fleet carrier, from the after hangar to the catapult forward. Note the large number of crewmen involved, including the Flight Deck Officer (FDO), walking behind the handling team. The photograph was probably taken on *Illustrious* during the late 1940s, which suggests it might be a crew training exercise.

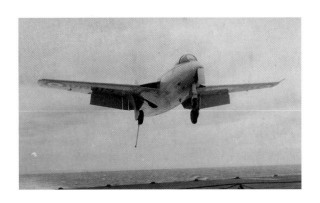

VP413, the prototype version of the Sea Hawk F1 piloted by Captain 'Winkle' Brown completing its landing on the flight deck of *Eagle* in 1952. This graceful little jet aircraft was much loved by its pilots, as it was a real joy to fly.

Four years later, the Fleet Air Arm was in action again during the Suez Crisis. When the British decided to react militarily to Nasser's takeover of the Suez Canal, *Albion*, *Bulwark* and *Eagle* formed the carrier strike force supporting the Anglo-French operation. They were accompanied by the French light carrier *Arromanches*, formerly the British *Colossus*. *Ocean* and *Theseus* were also there, but having been converted into commando carriers they only embarked helicopters, and were busy supporting the Royal Marines deployed ashore. This military intervention, codenamed Operation *Musketeer*, began on 30 October 1956 and lasted for a week, when a UN ceasefire was imposed. In that time, Sea Venoms from *Albion*'s 809 NAS attacked Egyptian airfields, a task then taken up by the Sea Hawks and Wyverns of other squadrons.

Reportedly, several Mig-15s were destroyed on the ground, but no aerial engagements took place. Two Wyverns and a Sea Hawk were shot down, but the pilots survived. The Sea Venoms also flew CAP missions over the fleet. Early on 5 November, three Egyptian fast-attack boats were spotted approaching the fleet as it lay off Port Said. The Sea Venoms of 893 NAS sank two of the Egyptian torpedo boats, leaving the third vessel to pick up survivors. This was probably the only air-to-sea action in defence of a naval force to take place since World War II.

In July 1961, *Bulwark*, now a commando carrier, was able to intervene when Iraq threatened to invade neighbouring Kuwait. In what was codenamed Operation *Vantage*, her embarked Royal Marine commandos were landed in Kuwait, and so helped to de-escalate the crisis. They were supported by the Wessex helicopters of 848 NAS. Ten days later, *Victorious* arrived, and the patrols flown by her Scimitars (803 NAS) and Sea Vixens (892 NAS) helped to encourage the Iraqis to back down. *Victorious* then headed south to Zanzibar, where she helped to deter local conflict between Arabs and Africans following an election in the small Sultanate. In the mid-1960s, British carriers were again deployed to the region, to help enforce UN

A Westland Wyvern S 4 (TF 4) torpedo bomber landing on a British fleet carrier (possibly *Eagle*) during the mid 1950s. *Eagle*'s Wyverns of 830 NAS saw action during the Suez Crisis (1956) in a ground-attack role, although they were not really designed for the task. Note the batsman on the carrier's port quarter, behind his screen. The batsmen were soon to be replaced by mirror landing aids.

sanctions against Rhodesia. In what became known as the Beira Patrol, British warships deterred tankers bound for the country, shipped there through the port of Beira in Mozambique. Both *Ark Royal* and *Eagle* took part in the Beira Patrol during 1965–66, tracking ships transiting the Mozambique Channel.

This post-colonial era also saw Britain's involvement in other brush wars, the most notable of which was the Borneo Confrontation (1963–66). The creation of Malaysia in 1963 from an amalgamation of Malaya, Sarawak and British Borneo led to an undeclared war with Indonesia, which opposed the union. British troops were sent to Borneo to protect the new country, and frequent jungle clashes took place as Indonesian incursions were repulsed. The Royal Navy and Royal Marines played their part in the conflict as the commando carriers *Albion* and *Bulwark* were sent to the region. Operating from bases in Sarawak, the Whirlwind and Wessex 1 helicopters of 845 NAS supported ground operations, until replaced by 845 NAS in 1964, flying the Wessex 5 commando helicopter. *Eagle*, *Centaur* and *Victorious* were also deployed in the region, although only the light carriers flew operational sorties, supported by the Australian light carrier *Melbourne*. *Centaur*'s Sea Vixens (892 NAS) flew anti-invasion patrols to deter Indonesian forays against the Malay Peninsula.

During this same period, British carriers were also active in the Gulf of Aden. In 1963, an Arab insurrection engulfed the Federation of South Arabia, a British protectorate which encompassed Aden. This developed into the Aden Emergency (1963–67), which ended with British withdrawal from the region, and the replacement of the Federation by the new, militant Arab state of South Yemen. Anti-British guerrilla groups were active in the Radfan Hills, and by 1967 this had spread to Aden itself. The Royal Navy and Royal Marines were involved in the Emergency, with both *Albion* and *Bulwark* being sent to Aden to spearhead anti-insurgency operations. *Centaur* and *Eagle* were also deployed in the Gulf of Aden during 1964–65, to fly strike missions over the Radfan. *Eagle* returned to Aden in 1967, to discourage tension in the port following the Arab-Israeli Six Day War.

G

TASK FORCE CARRIER BATTLE GROUP, FALKLANDS, 1982

Early on 2 April 1982, Argentina invaded the British Overseas Territory of the Falkland Islands. Argentina had long laid claim to the archipelago, regardless of the overwhelming wishes of the islanders. The British government responded to this unprovoked invasion by assembling a powerful naval task and land force, to send to the South Atlantic. The core of the Task Force was the Carrier Battle Group (Task Force 317.8), consisting of the light carriers *Hermes* and *Invincible*, together with escorts. *Hermes* also served as the flagship of the Task Force commander, Rear Admiral Sandy Woodward. On 1 May, the carriers reached their operating position 200nmi to the east-north-east of the Falklands. Their Sea Harriers had several tasks to perform including protecting the fleet and the subsequent British amphibious landings at San Carlos, also wresting air superiority over the archipelago from the Argentinians. They were remarkably successful and, despite claims to the contrary, the Argentinians were unable to damage the British carriers. Instead, 21 Argentinian aircraft were shot down by Sea Harriers for the combat loss of two of the V/STOL jets, both to ground fire. Four other Sea Harriers were lost in flying accidents during the war. In this scene, showing TF317.8, *Hermes* is launching and recovering her Sea Harriers, flying a Combat Air Patrol (CAP) mission, while in the distance, off her starboard beam, *Invincible* does the same. Also visible is one of the Carrier Battle Group's escorts, the County-class destroyer *Glamorgan*, tasked with anti-air protection for the carriers, using its long-range but outdated Sea Slug SAM system.

The Centaur-class light carrier *Albion* (RO7), off Aden 1960. At the time she carried Sea Hawks (806 NAS)and Sea Venoms (894 NAS), supported by Skyraider AEWs (849D NAS) and Wessex Is (815 NAS). She was on her way to join the Far Eastern Fleet, a deployment that lasted until the end of the year, when she was converted into a commando carrier.

The sleek lines of a Sea Hawk fighter jet, flying over her carrier, *Eagle* during an exercise with the Mediterranean Fleet in 1959. At the time she embarked Sea Hawks (802, 806 & 898 NAS), Gannets (814 NAS), Sea Venoms (894 NAS) and Skyraider AEWs (849A NAS).

Nevertheless, for the most part, the carriers of the post-war Royal Navy were deployed in support of NATO, conducting joint exercises with their NATO allies, and serving as a deterrent to any potential Soviet aggression. However, in April 1982 Britain found itself embroiled in a war on its own when Argentina invaded the Falkland Islands, a British overseas territory. The Argentinians had long coveted the archipelago, and talks had even taken place between the British and the Argentinians to discuss the transfer of the sovereignty of the islands, much against the wishes of the islanders. Following the invasion, a naval task force was assembled to spearhead the liberation of the Falklands. At its core was a Carrier Battle Group, consisting of *Hermes* and *Invincible*. Together they carried 31 Sea Harriers and 14 Sea Kings.

By late April, the British task force came within flying range of the Falkland Islands, and the two carriers began air operations. They had two primary missions: fleet air defence using the Sea Harriers and fleet anti-submarine protection using the Sea Kings. On 21 May the main British amphibious landing began at San Carlos in East Falkland. Although Argentinian military opposition was negligible, the landing was aggressively opposed by land-based strike aircraft from the Argentinian Air Force and its naval air wing, which pressed home repeated attacks against the Task Force in San Carlos Water, which the British soon nicknamed 'Bomb Alley'. For their part, the British defended the bay using the air defence weaponry of their ships, backed up by Rapier SAMs operated by army units ashore. More effectively though, Sea Harriers of the Carrier Strike Force were also on hand to protect the beachhead.

These V/STOL jets proved supremely effective, although they suffered from a lack of AEW, which would have helped them intercept Argentinian air attacks. This, together with more Sea Harriers, would have ensured better protection for the ships, and the establishment of complete air superiority over the islands. The loss of the container ship *Atlantic Conveyor* on 25 May, carrying 14 additional Sea Harriers and RAF Harriers had an impact on the ability of the carrier aircraft to protect the fleet fully. Still, despite warship losses, the amphibious landing was completed on 25 May, and as the troops pressed on inland the battered warships of the Task Force withdrew to the open sea, where they re-joined the Carrier Battle Group. The war finally ended on 14 June, following the recapture of the island's capital, Port Stanley, and the capitulation of the archipelago's Argentinian garrison.

During the war, the Fleet Air Arm's Sea Harriers shot down 32 Argentinian aircraft in air-to-air combat. Almost all of these confirmed kills were made by Sidewinder AAMs. Six Sea Harriers were shot down by ground fire, but notably none was lost in air combat. The aircraft emerged from the Falklands War as the real star of the operation. The aircraft's success did much to preserve Britain's carrier strike force for another two decades. Essentially, given the possibility of renewed Argentinian aggression, it was politically impossible to axe either the carriers or their V/STOL aircraft until both reached the end of their operational life. By then, of course, plans had been laid to replace the Invincible-class carriers and their Sea Harriers with a much more potent carrier strike force. However, their replacements have still to prove their effectiveness in action.

SHIP SPECIFICATIONS

Wartime carriers

Illustrious-class fleet carriers Three in class: *Illustrious, Victorious, Formidable*; details c. 1946	
Displacement	29,110–31,630 tons (fully laden)
Dimensions	length: 753ft 3in. overall, beam: 95ft 9in. at waterline, draught: 28ft 6in. (fully laden)
Propulsion	three shafts, three Parsons geared turbines, six Admiralty three-drum boilers, generating 111,000shp
Endurance	11,000 miles at 10kts
Maximum speed	30kts, fuel oil capacity 4,850 tons
Armament	16 4.5in./45 QF high-angle Mark III guns in eight twin mounts, 48 2pdr pom-poms in six eight-barrelled mounts, 16 20mm Oerlikons in single mounts
Protection	4.5in. belt, 3in. flight deck, 4.5in. hangar bulkheads, 2.5in. hangar deck
Aircraft facilities	flight deck length: 740ft, one hydraulic catapult
Hangar and lifts	456ft long served by two lifts
Aircraft capacity (c. 1946)	up to 36 aircraft, depending on type, or 54 if carried on deck using outriggers
Complement	1,997 (*Illustrious*: 1,090 as trials carrier)

Victorious, as modernized, c. 1956	
Displacement	3,550 tons (fully laden)
Dimensions	length: 778ft 3in. overall, beam: 95ft 9in. at waterline, draught: 31ft (fully laden)
Propulsion	three shafts, three Parsons geared turbines, six Admiralty three-drum boilers, generating 110,000shp.
Endurance	11,000 miles at 12kts
Maximum speed	31kts, fuel oil capacity 4,180 tons
Armament	12 US 3in. Mark 33 guns in six twin mounts, six 40mm Bofors in one six-barrelled mount
Protection	4.5in. belt, 3.5in. flight deck and hangar sides, 2.5in. hangar deck
Aircraft facilities	flight deck length: 775ft, angled deck of 8½°, two steam catapults
Hangar and lifts	412ft-long, hangar served by two lifts
Aircraft capacity (c.1956)	up to 36 aircraft, depending on type
Complement	2,400

Name	Built	Laid down	Launched	Completed	Fate
Illustrious	Vickers-Armstrong, Barrow-in-Furness	April 1937	April 1939	May 1940	Broken up 1956
Victorious	Vickers-Armstrong, Tyneside	May 1937	September 1939	May 1941	Broken up 1969
Formidable	Harland and Wolff, Belfast	June 1937	August 1939	November 1940	Broken up 1953

Illustrious

Illustrious had an impressive wartime career, including launching the raid on Taranto (1940). She ended the war in the British Pacific Fleet. Post-war, she served as a trials carrier. Placed in reserve in 1954, *Illustrious* was sold for scrap in 1956.

Victorious

Victorious' wartime career included attacks on both *Bismarck* and *Tirpitz*, before joining the British Pacific Fleet. Damaged in kamikaze attacks, she was repaired in Australia. She underwent a major refit from 1950 to 1958, emerging with an angled flight deck suitable for the operation of modern jets. Further refits in 1960 and 1967 followed. During the latter, damage from a fire resulted in the decision not to re-commission her. She was sold for scrap in 1969.

Formidable

Formidable participated in the Battle of Matapan (1941) and ended the war in the British Pacific Fleet, where she was damaged in a kamikaze attack. Placed in reserve in 1947, she was sold off in 1953, and scrapped in 1956.

Indomitable-class fleet carrier One in class: *Indomitable*	
Displacement	29,730 tons (fully laden)
Dimensions	length: 753ft 11in. overall, beam: 95ft 9in. at waterline, draught: 29ft fully laden
Propulsion	three shafts, three Parsons geared turbines, six Admiralty three-drum boilers, generating 111,000shp.
Maximum speed	30½kts, fuel oil capacity 4,500 tons
Endurance	9,000 miles at 18kts
Armament	sixteen 4.5in/45 QF high-angle Mark III guns in eight twin mounts, 48 2pdr pom-poms in six eight-barrelled mounts, 12 40mm Bofors in single mounts, 16 20mm Oerlikons in single mounts
Protection	4.5in. belt, 3in. flight deck, 1.5in. hangar bulkheads, 2.5in. over magazines
Aircraft facilities	flight deck length: 745ft, one hydraulic catapult
Hangar and lifts	416ft-long upper hangar, 168ft-long lower hangar served by two lifts (forward one serving upper hangar only)
Aircraft capacity (c.1946)	up to 36 aircraft, depending on type, or 56 if carried on deck using outriggers
Complement	2,100

Name	Built	Laid down	Launched	Completed	Fate
Indomitable	Vickers-Armstrong, Barrow-in-Furness	November 1937	March 1940	October 1941	Broken up 1955

Indomitable

Indomitable saw action during the Malta Convoy operations, and was damaged during Operation *Pedestal* (1942), off Sicily (1943) and by kamikazes in the Pacific (1945). She remained in service until sold for scrap in 1953.

Implacable-class fleet carriers
Two in class: *Implacable, Indefatigable*

Displacement	32,110 tons (fully laden)
Dimensions	length: 766ft 4in. overall, beam: 95ft 9in. at waterline, draught: 28ft 11in. fully laden
Propulsion	four shafts, four Parsons geared turbines, eight Admiralty three-drum boilers, generating 148,000shp.
Maximum speed	32kts
Fuel oil capacity	*Implacable*: 4,690 tons, *Indefatigable*: 4,810 tons
Endurance	12,000 miles at 10kts
Armament	sixteen 4.5in/45 QF high-angle Mark III guns in eight twin mounts, 44 2pdr pom-poms in five eight-barrelled and one quadruple mounts, 12 40mm Bofors in single mounts, 16 20mm Oerlikons in single mounts
Protection	4.5in. belt, 3in. flight deck, 25in. hangar bulkheads and sides, 3in. over magazines, with 4.5in. sides
Aircraft facilities	flight deck length: 760ft, one hydraulic catapult
Hangar and lifts	456ft-long upper hangar, 208ft-long lower hangar served by two lifts (forward one serving upper hangar only)
Aircraft capacity (c.1946)	up to 48 aircraft, depending on type, or 81 if carried on deck using outriggers
Complement	2,300

Name	Built	Laid down	Launched	Completed	Fate
Implacable	Fairfield, Clydebank	February 1939	December 1942	August 1944	Broken up 1955
Indefatigable	John Brown, Clydeside	November 1939	December 1942	May 1944	Broken up 1956

Implacable

Implacable ended the war in the British Pacific Fleet and was refitted in 1948–49, then primarily served as a training carrier until 1952–1954. She was placed in reserve in 1954, and sold off for scrap in 1955.

Indefatigable

Indefatigable ended the war in the British Pacific Fleet and was placed in reserve from 1946 until 1949, then used as a training carrier from 1950–1954. In 1954 she was sold for scrap.

The light carrier *Eagle*, pictured in 1956–57. The partially angled flight deck seen here was fitted in 1955–56, together with two steam catapults and a mirror landing system. Ranged on deck in this photograph are Sea Hawks (including two on her catapults), with Wyverns farther aft.

Eagle-class fleet carriers
Two in class: *Eagle* **and** *Ark Royal*; **one more was broken up while still under construction, 1946**

As commissioned	
Displacement	49,950 tons (fully laden)
Dimensions	length: 803ft 9in. overall, beam: 112ft 9in. at waterline, draught: 31ft 1in. (fully laden)
Propulsion	four shafts, four Parsons geared turbines, eight Admiralty three-drum boilers, generating 152,000shp.
Maximum speed	32kts, fuel oil capacity 7,490 tons
Endurance	7,000nm at 14kts
Armament	sixteen 4.5in/45 QF high-angle Mark III guns in eight twin mounts, 57 40mm Bofors in eight six-barrelled and nine single mounts
Protection	4.5in. belt, 1.5–4in. flight deck, 1.5–2.5in. hangar deck, 1.5in. hangar sides
Aircraft facilities	flight deck length: 800ft, two hydraulic catapults
Hangar and lifts	409ft-long upper hangar, 172ft-long lower hangar served by two lifts
Aircraft capacity (as designed)	up to 100 aircraft, depending on type
Complement	2,750

Eagle, as modernized, c. 1964

Displacement	50,536 tons (fully laden)
Dimensions	length: 813ft 5in. overall, beam: 112ft 9in. at waterline, draught: 34ft 6in. (fully laden)
Propulsion	four shafts, four Parsons geared turbines, eight Admiralty three-drum boilers, generating 152,000shp
Maximum speed	30½kts, fuel oil capacity: 3,200 tons
Endurance	7,000nm at 14kts
Armament	eight 4.5in/45 QF high-angle Mark III guns in four twin mounts, six GWS-22 quadruple Seacat SAMs
Protection	4.5in. belt, 1.5–4in. flight deck, 1.5–2.5in. hangar deck, 1.5in. hangar sides
Aircraft facilities: flight deck length: 800ft, angled deck of 8°, two steam catapults	
Hangar and lifts	409ft-long upper hangar, 172ft-long lower hangar, served by two lifts
Aircraft capacity (c.1964)	up to 44 aircraft, depending on type
Complement	2,750

Ark Royal, as modernized, c.1970

Displacement	50,786 tons (fully laden)
Dimensions	length: 845ft overall, beam: 112ft 9in. at waterline, draught: 36ft (fully laden)
Propulsion	four shafts, four Parsons geared turbines, eight Admiralty three-drum boilers, generating 152,000shp
Maximum speed	30½kts, fuel oil capacity: 5,500 tons
Endurance	7,000nm at 14kts
Armament	none fitted
Protection	4.5in. belt, 1.5–4in. flight deck, 1.5–2.5in. hangar deck, 1.5in. hangar sides
Aircraft facilities	flight deck length: 790ft angled deck of 8½°, two steam catapults
Hangar and lifts	409ft-long upper hangar, 172ft-long lower hangar, served by two lifts.
Aircraft capacity (c.1975)	up to 38 aircraft, depending on type
Complement	2,640

Name	Built	Laid down	Launched	Completed	Fate
Eagle (formerly Audacious)	Harland and Wolff, Belfast	October 1942	March 1946	October 1951	Broken up, 1978
Ark Royal	Cammell Laird, Merseyside	May 1943	May 1950	February 1955	Broken up, 1979
Eagle	Vickers-Armstrong, Tyneside	April 1944	–	–	Cancelled 1946 and broken up

Eagle

Eagle was accepted into service in 1952, on completion of flying trials. She served in home waters and the Mediterranean (1952–54), before undergoing a refit (1954–55). This saw the addition of an angled flight deck and mirror landing aids. On re-commissioning, she was deployed both in home and Mediterranean waters (1954–56). In 1956 *Eagle* served during the Suez Crisis. A major refit followed (1959–64), which included improvements to the angled flight deck, the addition of steam catapults and an extensive electronics suite. She underwent another refit in 1966–67, but plans to fit jet deflectors were shelved, which meant that she was unable to operate F4 Phantoms. *Eagle* remained in active service until 1972, when she was placed in reserve. She was sold for scrap in 1978.

Ark Royal

Ark Royal served in home waters in 1955–56, and although earmarked to participate in the Suez Crisis (1956), mechanical problems prevented her involvement. She undertook trials of V/STOL aircraft in 1963, before service on the Beira Patrol off East Africa in 1965. NATO service in home waters and the Mediterranean followed (1966–78), and her aircraft patrolled over Belize in 1972 to deter a Guatemalan military threat. Decommissioned in 1979, *Ark Royal* was sold for scrap in 1980.

After her major refit of 1950-58, the profile of HMS *Eagle* (R05) was dominated by her dustbin-shaped Type 984 3D Air Search radar, mounted above her bridge. The same radar system was also fitted in *Victorious* and *Hermes*. Aft of it is the 'bedstead' Type 965 radar. This picture, of her was taken in 1965, in the Indian Ocean and shows Buccaneers (800 NAS) ranged on deck.

Unicorn-class light fleet carrier
One in class: *Unicorn*, in service 1957–65. Six in this class were built, but one was broken up incomplete, and four more were commissioned into Commonwealth navies on completion.

Displacement	20,300 tons (fully laden)
Dimensions	length: 646ft overall, beam: 90ft, draught: 24ft (fully laden)
Propulsion	two shafts, two Parsons geared turbines, four Admiralty three-drum boilers, generating 40,000shp
Maximum speed	24kts, fuel oil capacity: 3,000 tons
Endurance	7,500nm at 20kts
Armament	eight 4in./45 QF HA Mark XVI guns in four twin mounts, 16 2pdr pom-poms in four quadruple mounts
Protection	2in. on flight deck and over magazines, 4–4.5in. on magazine sides, 1.25in. anti-torpedo bulkhead
Aircraft facilities	flight deck length: 640ft, one hydraulic catapult
Hangar and lifts	329ft-long hangar, served by two lifts
Aircraft capacity (as designed)	up to 35 aircraft, depending on type as operational carrier, 24 if undergoing repairs or 80 if being ferried
Complement	1,200

Name	Built	Laid down	Launched	Completed	Fate
Unicorn	Harland and Wolff, Belfast	June 1939	November 1941	March 1943	Broken up, 1959

Unicorn

Built as a depot maintenance ship, *Unicorn* saw action off Salerno (1943), and ended World War II in the British Pacific Fleet. Placed in reserve from 1946 to 1949, *Unicorn* was then used as an aircraft transport carrier during the Korean War, as well as fulfilling troopship, maintenance and resupply roles during the conflict. Placed in reserve in 1953, she was sold for scrap in 1959.

Colossus-class light fleet carriers
In service 1945–62
Eight in class: *Colossus, Glory, Ocean, Venerable, Vengeance, Theseus, Triumph* and *Warrior*
Two more, *Perseus* and *Pioneer*, were completed in 1945 as aircraft maintenance ships.

Displacement	18,040 tons (fully laden) (*Theseus, Triumph* and *Warrior*: 18,300 tons)
Dimensions	length: 693–695ft overall, beam: 80ft at waterline, draught: 23ft 3in. (fully laden)
Propulsion	two shafts, two Parsons geared turbines, four Admiralty three-drum boilers, generating 40,000shp
Maximum speed	25kts, fuel oil capacity: 3,196 tons
Endurance	8,300nm at 20kts (*Pioneer* and *Perseus*: 8,500nm at 11kts)
Armament (as commissioned)	varied, but typically 16 2pdr pom-poms in six quadruple mounts, 16 40mm Bofors in single mounts. Instead of this, *Pioneer* and *Perseus* were fitted with 16 20mm Oerlikons in single mounts
Aircraft facilities	flight deck length: 690ft, one hydraulic catapult (except in *Pioneer* and *Perseus*)
Hangar and lifts	332ft-long hangar, served by two centreline lifts, 275ft in *Pioneer* and *Perseus*
Aircraft capacity (as designed)	up to 42 aircraft, depending on type, except *Pioneer* and *Perseus*, which could carry up to 20 aircraft under repair or 60 being ferried
Complement	1,300

Name	Built	Laid down	Launched	Completed	Fate
Colossus	Vickers-Armstrong, Tyneside	June 1942	September 1943	December 1944	Transferred to France, 1946
Glory	Harland and Wolff, Belfast	August 1942	November 1943	April 1945	Broken up, 1961
Ocean	Stephen, Clydeside	November 1942	July 1944	August 1945	Broken up, 1962
Venerable	Cammell Laird, Merseyside	December 1942	December 1943	January 1945	Transferred to the Netherlands, 1946
Vengeance	Swan Hunter, Tyneside	November 1942	February 1944	January 1945	Transferred to Brazil, 1956
Theseus	Fairfield, Clydeside	January 1943	July 1944	February 1946	Broken up, 1962
Triumph	Hawthorn Leslie, Tyneside	January 1943	October 1944	May 1946	Repair ship, 1964
Warrior	Harland and Wolff, Belfast	December 1942	May 1944	March 1946	Transferred to Argentina, 1958
Perseus	Vickers-Armstrong, Tyneside	June 1942	March 1944	October 1945	Aircraft maintenance ship
Pioneer	Vickers-Armstrong, Barrow-in-Furness	December 1942	May 1944	February 1945	Aircraft maintenance ship

Colossus

Colossus joined the British Pacific Fleet too late to see action in World War II. In 1946, she was transferred on loan to the French Navy, becoming the carrier *Arromanches*. She was officially sold to France in 1951 and remained in service until 1974. She was sold for scrap in 1978.

Glory

Like *Colossus*, *Glory* joined the British Pacific Fleet too late to see action. However, she did repatriate former POWs. Placed in reserve between1947 and 1950, she was then re-commissioned, and between 1950 and 1952, saw service during the Korean War and in the Malay Emergency. Placed in reserve in 1956, she was sold for scrap in 1961.

Ocean

Ocean was also commissioned too late to see action, but in December 1945 she was used in the first jet carrier landing. After a refit in 1947, she was used as a supply carrier ship during 1948 and 1949 and then saw service off Korea (1950–53). During the Suez Crisis (1956) she was used as a commando carrier. Placed in reserve in 1957, she was sold for scrap in 1960.

The Colossus-class light carrier *Ocean* (R68), pictured during her deployment to Korea in 1952. That May she broke the FAA record for the most sorties in a single day, dropping 90 tons of ordnance. Pictured on her flight deck are her embarked Sea Furies (802 NAS) and Fireflies (825 NAS). She also carried two Dragonfly SAR helicopters.

Venerable

Venerable also joined the British Pacific Fleet too late to see action. Placed in reserve in 1947, she was sold to the Royal Netherlands Navy in 1948, becoming the *Karel Doorman*. Retained by the Dutch until 1967, she was then sold to Argentina, becoming the *Veinticinco de Mayo*. She was refitted with an angled flight deck and steam catapult in 1981. In the following year, she was used against Britain during the Falklands War (1982). Decommissioned in 1998, she was sold for scrap in 2000.

Vengeance

Vengeance also joined the British Pacific Fleet too late to see action. Instead, she was used to repatriate former POWs, and used as a supply carrier. From 1947 to 1950 she served in the Home Fleet, conducting cold-weather trials for helicopters in Arctic waters. After being lent to the Australian Navy from 1952 to 1955, she was then decommissioned. In 1956, she was sold to the Brazilian Navy in 1956 and modernized in the Netherlands from 1956 to 1960, receiving an angled flight deck. On completion, she became the *Minais Gerais*, and remained in Brazilian service until 2001, when she was decommissioned. She was sold for scrap in 2004.

Theseus

Theseus served in the Far East from 1946 to 1947, then in the Home Fleet from 1948 to 1950, when she was refitted. In 1950, she trialled jet carrier landings at night and saw service during the Korean War (1950–51). *Theseus* rejoined the Home Fleet, but returned to Korea as part of a UN task force from 1952 to 1953. Refitted in 1954, she was used as a training carrier until 1956, when she saw action off Suez as a commando carrier. She briefly resumed a training role in 1957, before being placed in reserve that October. She was sold for scrap in 1962.

Triumph

Triumph served with the Home and Mediterranean Fleets from 1946 to 1949, before being deployed to the Far East. She saw action during the Malay Emergency in 1949 and the Korean War from 1950 to 1951, being the first British carrier to arrive in Korean waters. She was used for trials and training (1952–53), including the evaluation of angled flight deck designs. *Triumph* served as a cadet training ship (1953–56), before being placed in reserve (1956–61). After conversion into a repair ship (1962–65), she saw service in the Far East, including providing support during the Indonesian Confrontation in 1965. Placed in reserve in 1973, she was sold for scrap in 1980.

Warrior

Warrior was transferred on loan to the Canadian Navy on completion in 1946, and returned in 1948. She was refitted specifically to evaluate the flexible flight deck, with trials continuing through 1948 and 1949, then placed in reserve on completion, but recommissioned in 1950 because of the Korean War. *Warrior* was employed as a transport carrier from 1950 to 1951 before undergoing an extensive refit over the next two years. On completion, she saw service in Korean waters (1954–55), before returning home for another refit, this time to evaluate the angled flight deck. Subsequently, she served as a training ship in 1956 and was deployed to the Far East to support hydrogen bomb tests in 1957. *Warrior* was decommissioned in 1958 and sold to the Argentinian navy, becoming the *Independencia*. She remained in service until 1970, then placed in reserve and sold for scrap in 1971.

Perseus

Perseus was completed as a maintenance carrier, but was subsequently used as a trials and transport carrier. In 1950, she was fitted with an experimental steam catapult for evaluation purposes and trials lasted until 1952. Converted into a transport carrier, she fulfilled that role until 1954 and was then used to test ASW helicopter operations, before resuming transport duties. She was placed in reserve in 1954 and sold for scrap in 1958.

Pioneer

Completed as a maintenance carrier, *Pioneer* served with the British Pacific Fleet during the closing months of World War II. Placed in reserve in 1946, she was sold for scrap in 1954.

Post-war carriers

Centaur-class light fleet carriers Four in class: *Albion, Bulwark, Centaur, Hermes* Four others: *Arrogant, Hermes, Monmouth* and *Polyphemus* were cancelled in 1945 without being laid down.	
Centaur specifications	
Displacement	27,800 tons (fully laden)
Dimensions	length: 737ft overall, beam: 90ft at waterline, draught: 24ft 8in. (fully laden)
Propulsion	two shafts, two Parsons geared turbines, four Admiralty three-drum boilers, generating 76,000shp
Maximum speed	28kts, fuel oil capacity: 3,500 tons
Endurance	5,000nm at 20kts
Armament	ten 40mm Bofors in four twin and two single mounts
Protection	1–2in. on flight deck, 1in. above magazines and funnel uptakes
Aircraft facilities	flight deck length: 733ft, two steam catapults (hydraulic catapults on *Albion*)
Hangar and lifts	329ft-long hangar, served by two lifts
Aircraft capacity (as designed)	up to 42 aircraft, depending on type
Complement	1,390
Hermes specifications c.1968	
Displacement	27,800 tons (fully laden)
Dimensions	length: 774ft overall, beam: 90ft at waterline, draught: 24ft 8in. (fully laden)
Propulsion	two shafts, two Parsons geared turbines, four Admiralty three-drum boilers, generating 76,000shp
Maximum speed	28kts, fuel oil capacity; 3,500 tons

Endurance	5,000nm at 20kts
Armament	two quadruple GWS-22 Seacat SAMs
Protection	1–2in. on flight deck, 1in. above magazines and funnel uptakes
Aircraft facilities	flight deck length: 744ft, angled deck of 8°, two steam catapults
Hangar and lifts	356ft-long hangar, served by two lifts
Aircraft capacity (as designed)	up to 30 aircraft, depending on type
Complement	2,100

Name	Built	Laid down	Launched	Completed	Fate
Albion	Swan Hunter, Tyneside	March 1944	May 1947	May 1954	Broken up, 1972
Bulwark	Harland and Wolff, Belfast	May 1945	June 1948	November 1954	Broken up, 1984
Centaur	Harland and Wolff, Belfast	May 1944	February 1953	September 1953	Broken up, 1972
Hermes (formerly Elephant)	Cammell Laird, Merseyside	June 1944	February 1953	November 1959	Sold to India, 1986, becoming Vikrant. Broken up, 2021

Albion

Commissioned in 1954, *Albion* subsequently saw action during the Suez Crisis (1956). She later served in the Far East, before her conversion into a commando carrier (1961–62). In this guise she saw action during the Indonesian Confrontation, and again off Aden. Another deployment to the Far East followed, then exercises in home waters. She was decommissioned later that year and scrapped in 1973.

Bulwark

Like Albion, *Bulwark* first saw action during the Suez Crisis (1956). She was converted into a commando carrier (1958–61), and saw service off Borneo during the Indonesian Confrontation. Nicknamed 'The Rusty B', she saw extensive service during the next two decades, but in 1976 she was placed in reserve, then eventually refitted as an ASW carrier (1978–79). She remained in service until damaged by a major fire in 1981, at which point she was decommissioned, then scrapped three years later.

Centaur

Primarily deployed on overseas service, *Centaur* served in the Mediterranean (1954–55), then the Indian Ocean and the Far East (1956). After modernization (1956–58), she returned to the Mediterranean (1958–59), and was used for the filming of *Sink the Bismarck! Centaur* then returned to the Indian Ocean, before returning home for another refit. Between 1961 and 1966, she served in the Indian Ocean and the Far East, and saw action during the Indonesian Confrontation. She was decommissioned in 1966, and scrapped six years later.

Hermes

After commissioning in 1959, *Hermes* was often deployed in the Indian Ocean and the Far East. In 1964, a planned upgrade to carry F-4 Phantoms was abandoned after trials. Instead, she operated

The light carrier *Centaur* pictured while passing through the Panama Canal in 1959. She had just completed a refit which saw her fitted with steam catapults. She already had a partially-angled flight deck, fitted just after she was commissioned in 1953. *Centaur* would remain in service until 1965 – a relatively short operational life for a carrier of her class.

Buccaneers as strike aircraft, supported by Sea Vixens until 1970–72, when she was converted into a commando carrier. In 1976, she was converted into an ASW carrier, a function she retained until 1980–81, when she was modified to carry the Sea Harrier. During the Falklands War (1982), *Hermes* was the flagship of the British Task Force, and her aircraft played a major part in the conflict. In 1983, she was placed in reserve and decommissioned in 1984, before being sold to the Indian Navy two years later. She duly served for two more decades as the INS *Vikraat*, until she was finally retired from service in 2017. She was scrapped in 2021.

Invincible-class light aircraft carrier Three in class: *Invincible, Illustrious, Ark Royal*	
Displacement	19,500 tons (fully laden)
Dimensions	length: 689ft overall, beam: 118ft, 1in. at waterline, draught: 28ft 10in. (fully laden)
Propulsion	two shafts, four Rolls-Royce Olympus TM3B gas turbines, eight Paxman Valenta diesel generators, generating 112,000shp
Maximum speed	28kts, fuel oil capacity: 3,000 tons
Endurance	5,000 nm at 18kts
Armament	one twin GWS-30 Sea Dart SAM, three Phalanx-Goalkeeper CIWS, two single Oerlikon 20mm mounts
Aircraft facilities	flight deck length: 551ft, 7° ski jump (*Ark Royal*: 12°)
Hangar and lifts	500ft-long hangar, served by two lifts
Aircraft capacity (as designed)	up to 20 aircraft, depending on type
Complement	1,100

Name	Built	Laid down	Launched	Commissioned	Fate
Invincible	Vickers-Armstrong, Barrow-in-Furness	July 1973	May 1977	July 1980	Broken up, 2011
Illustrious	Swan Hunter, Tyneside	October 1976	December 1978	June 1982	Broken up, 2017
Ark Royal	Swan Hunter, Tyneside	December 1978	June 1981	November 1985	Broken up, 2013

Invincible

In 1981, during NATO exercises, *Invincible* was able to demonstrate the potential of her embarked air wing of Sea Harriers and Sea Kings. However, the government decided to sell her to the Australian Navy – a scheme which was thwarted by the Falklands War in 1982. Together with *Hermes*, *Invincible* formed the British Carrier Battle Group in the South Atlantic, and played a major part in liberating the Falklands. Subsequently, as fleet flagship she was deployed to the Far East, and then to the Mediterranean and Adriatic, where she covered UN operations in former Yugoslavia. In 2005 she was placed in reserve, and used as a source of spare parts for her sister ships. She was finally stricken from the fleet list in 2010, and scrapped the following year.

Illustrious

'*Lusty*' was being fitted out when the Falklands War began; she was hurriedly completed, and sailed for the South Atlantic in July 1982. Although *Illustrious* arrived too late to participate in the war, she helped to defend the islands until the RAF could establish a viable airbase there. She then sailed to the Caribbean to conduct exercises, before returning to Britain. During the decade that followed, *Illustrious* was modified to carry a steeper ski jump ramp, and a larger air wing. She was subsequently deployed to the Far East, and then to the Mediterranean, to maintain a no-fly zone over Bosnia, and in 2006, assisted humanitarian efforts off Lebanon. On 11 September 2011, she was deployed to the Persian Gulf and remained in active service until 2014, when she was decommissioned and scrapped two years later.

Ark Royal

During the late 1980s, the carrier was deployed in the North Atlantic, participating in numerous NATO exercises. In 1988, she was deployed to the Far East, where she operated with the Australian Navy. From 1988 to 1990 she resumed operations with NATO, before being redeployed to the Adriatic to help enforce the no-fly zone over Bosnia. After a refit (1999–2001), she was deployed in the Persian Gulf (2003), before undergoing another refit (2004–06). Further service with NATO followed, before she was decommissioned in 2010. *Ark Royal* was scrapped in 2013.

FURTHER READING

Beaver, Paul, *Encyclopedia of the Fleet Air Arm since 1945*, Patrick Stephens Ltd, Yeovil, 1987

——, *The British Aircraft Carrier*, Patrick Stephens Ltd, Yeovil, 1987

Bond, Stephen, *Fleet Air Arm Boys Volume 1: Air Defence Fighter Aircraft since 1945*, Grub Street Publishing, London, 2020

——, *Fleet Air Arm Boys Volume 2: Strike, Anti-Submarine, Early Warning and Support Aircraft since 1945*, Grub Street Publishing, London, 2021

Brown, David, *The Royal Navy and the Falklands War*, Leo Cooper Ltd, London, 1987

Chesneau, Robert, *Aircraft Carriers of the World, 1914 to the Present: An Illustrated Encyclopedia*, Arms & Armour Press, London, 1984

Darling, Kev, *Fleet Air Arm Carrier War: The History of British Naval Aviation*, Pen & Sword, Barnsley, 2009

Friedman, Norman, *British Carrier Aviation: The Evolution of the Ships and their Aircraft*, Conway Maritime Press, London, 1988

—— (ed.), *Conway's All the World's Fighting Ships, 1947–1995*, Naval Institute Press, Annapolis, MD, 1996

——, *Fighters over the Fleet: Naval Air Defence from Biplanes to the Cold War*, Seaforth Publishing, Barnsley, 2016

Gardiner, Robert (ed.), *Conway's All the World's Fighting Ships, 1922–1946*, Conway Maritime Press, London, 1980

—— (ed.), *Conway's All the World's Fighting Ships, 1947–1982, Part 1: The Western Powers*, Conway Maritime Press, London, 1983

——, *Navies in the Nuclear Age: Warships since 1945*, Conway Maritime Press, London, 1993 [Conway's History of the Ship series]

Hobbs, David, *British Aircraft Carriers: Design, Development & Service Histories*, Seaforth Publishing, Barnsley, 2013

——, *The British Carrier Strike Fleet after 1945*, Seaforth Publishing, Barnsley, 2015

Tillman, Barrett, *On Wave and Wing: The 100-Year Quest to Improve the Aircraft Carrier*, Regnery History, Washington DC, 2017

Watton, Ross, *The Aircraft Carrier* Victorious, Conway Maritime Press, London, 1991 [Anatomy of the Ship series]

INDEX